IBIZA AND
FORMENTERA

BY
CHRISTOPHER AND MELANIE RICE

Produced by
Thomas Cook Publishing

Written by Christopher and Melanie Rice

Original photography by Caroline Jones

Original design by Laburnum Technologies Pvt Ltd

Editing and page layout by Cambridge Publishing Management Limited, 149B Histon Road, Cambridge CB4 3JD

Published by Thomas Cook Publishing
A division of Thomas Cook Tour Operations Limited

PO Box 227, The Thomas Cook Business Park, Unit 15/16, Coningsby Road, Peterborough PE3 8SB, United Kingdom
E-mail: books@thomascook.com
www.thomascookpublishing.com

ISBN: 1-841573-86-8

Text © 2004 Thomas Cook Publishing
Maps © 2004 Thomas Cook Publishing
First edition © 2004 Thomas Cook Publishing

Head of Thomas Cook Publishing: Donald Greig
Project Editor: Charlotte Christensen
Project Administrator: Michelle Warrington
DTP: Steven Collins

Printed and bound in Spain by: Grafo Industrias Gráficas, Basauri

Cover: Ibiza Town. Photograph by Jon Arnold Images/Alamy
Inside cover: All photos by Brand X Pictures/Alamy, except bottom left by ImageGap/Alamy

CD manufacturing services provided by business interactive ltd, Rutland, UK
CD edited and designed by Laburnum Technologies Pvt Ltd.

Contents

Introduction

To the Phoenicians, Ibiza was a magic island, blessed by the gods. They came here to bury their dead because there were no poisonous snakes or other creatures harmful to man. Ibiza was prized by the Carthaginians, who extracted salt from the pans near today's international airport, and by the Romans, who found the soil of Formentera well-suited to growing crops. For the Moors, too, Ibiza was a land of plenty; they introduced revolutionary agricultural techniques still discernible today in the marshes of Ses Feixes. The Catalans saw Ibiza as a forward base in the Mediterranean, ripe for economic exploitation.

Sunrise over Eivissa

But it was the Ibizan landscape, and a way of life that had changed little over the centuries, that captivated the Beat Generation writers William Burroughs and Jack Kerouac in the 1950s. Folk singer Bob Dylan arrived a decade later. In his wake came the hippies, who found a Garden of Eden unsullied by material values and bad karma. They explored the island's hidden reaches in search of mystical secrets and banged their drums in homage to the setting sun at Benniràs.

Much has changed in the last 50 years. Mass tourism, which now accounts for nearly two million visitors a year, has left an indelible mark on Ibizan society. It has generated a great deal of wealth (the residents of Santa Eulària have the highest income per capita in Spain), but large tracts of coastline have been sacrificed to insensitive urban development in the process. The image many have today, of eyesore hotels and soulless apartment blocks, of hordes of British and German tourists packing the beaches by day and the bars by night, is not an unfounded one. But neither is it wholly fair or accurate. There is a lot

Beguiling courtyard in Dalt Vila

more to Ibiza than burger bars and cut-price beer. Eivissa, the capital, is a lively town with a cosmopolitan feel and boasts a World Heritage Site in Dalt Vila, the walled city founded more than two and a half millennia ago. Sant Antoni is where the young come to party, dancing the night – or sometimes the day – away in Space, Eden or Es Paradis. 'San An' too offers more than foam parties and Manumission, not least the

wonderful bay which boasts three 'blue flag' beaches. Sedate Santa Eulària is for those who want to give the hectic clubbing scene a wide berth. Visitors are charmed by the stark simplicity of its fortified church, built in the 16th century to ward off pirate attacks.

Not all of Ibiza's coastline is developed. With 56 beaches at the last count, there is still plenty of scope for discovering a remote cove in the shelter of a lowering cliff, or a patch of fine white sand backed by dunes and sabine pines. During the last decade, whole swathes of the Pitiusas have acquired protected status. The largest Natural Park is Ses Salines, 2,000 acres of wetland and coastal waters around

Ibiza and Formentera. Within its confines are numerous hiking and cycling trails and untold opportunities for birdwatching – more than 200 species have been recorded to date. Visitors looking for peace and quiet will find solitude in the pine-forested hills of Els Amunts and Sant Josep or on the terraced slopes of the Corona plain. They will also discover why Ibiza is sometimes referred to as the 'white island': the hillsides are peppered with *casaments*, lime-washed cottages modelled on an Arab design more than a thousand years old and never bettered, as the revolutionary modern architect, Le Corbusier, was quick to recognise. For genuine lovers of the island, this unspoilt 'other Ibiza' is the real one.

Land

Ibiza and Formentera form part of an archipelago which is situated southwest of Mallorca and about 170km (106 miles) east of the Spanish mainland. From the time of the ancient Greeks, they have been known as the Pitiusas or 'pine islands'. There are more than 50 in all, though most are uninhabited. Ibiza, the largest island in the group, has an area of 572sq km (221sq miles) and a 210km (131 mile)-long coastline. Formentera is only 14km (9 miles) long from west to east, with a total area of 82sq km (32sq miles).

'Atlantis' the name given by hippies to the quarry near Torre d'es Savinar

Landscape

There are two uplands in Ibiza, clearly visible as your aeroplane flies overhead. The Serra de Els Amunts stretches all the way from Cala Sant Vicent on the northeast coast to Cala Salada in the west. Ibiza's highest peak, Sa Talaiassa (476m (0.3 mile)), rises not here but among the pine-covered hills of the Serra de Sant Josep in the southwest. The best farming land, characterised by a reddish clay soil, lies in the depression between the two ranges. The rugged coastline to the west of Els Amunts, roughly from Cap Nonó to Cap d'Aubarca, is wild and inaccessible in places and consequently free of tourist development. By contrast, the sandy coves and beaches in the south and east have been heavily promoted, turning the ancient settlements of Santa Eulària, Sant Antoni and Eivissa into major holiday destinations. The wetlands in the southeast corner are of great ecological importance and form part of the Ses Salines Natural Park.

The topography of Formentera is relatively straightforward. Two plateaus, one to the south (Barbària), the other at La Mola, are joined by a narrow isthmus with dunes and white sand beaches on either side. The salt lagoons of Estany Pudent and Estany de Peix are included in the Ses Salines Natural Park. Other features include a number of offshore islands and Es Trucadors, a finger-like promontory with more stunning beaches backed by dunes and pine woods.

Climate

Ibiza and Formentera have a Mediterranean climate with long, hot summers – warmer than Mallorca – and mild winters. Temperatures range from a daily average of 15°C (59°F) between November and April, to 29°C (84°F) in August. Sunshine levels are also high, with an average of 10 or 11 hours from May to September, and rarely fewer than 5 hours in November and December. Cooling afternoon breezes tend to mitigate the high summer temperatures, which only really cause discomfort when the hot, dry wind known as the *leveche* blows in from Africa. Rainfall is moderate, the wettest months being March (51mm (2 inches)) and October (77mm (3 inches)). Virtually no rain falls in July. There is relatively little fluctuation in sea temperatures, which range from a high of 25°C (77°F) in August down to 13°C (55°F) in February.

Flora and fauna

Ibiza's southern latitude determines its flora and fauna. The ubiquitous pines, sabines and wild olive trees flourish on the upper hillsides, while on the lower slopes are junipers and rock roses. The rich soils of the central plains and valleys are ideally suited to the growing of olives, figs, vines, carobs (the fruit of the algarroba tree) and a variety of citrus fruits. Almonds are a speciality of the Santa Agnès plain, where blossom falls in January and February to create a snowscape effect. Bougainvillea, oleander and hibiscus all come into flower from July to September, adding more than a splash of colour, while cacti, agaves and palms thrive all year round. Rosemary, thyme and wild fennel are among the herbs used to season traditional Ibizan dishes. Numerous autochthonous plants are protected by environmental legislation, for example the *crithmum maritinum* which grows on Es Vedrà. The soil on Formentera is not as productive because of the erosion caused by winds sweeping across the countryside during winter. Even here, though, vines, carobs and figs grow around El Mola and along the central

Sabine pines and wild olive trees are a feature of the Ibizan landscape

The unruffled waters of the Ses Salines salt pans

isthmus, while clumps of rosemary and thyme can be found even in the wildest reaches of the Barbària peninsula. The Ses Salines salt marshes in Eivissa and the salt lagoons of Formentera form an ecosystem unique to the Pitiusas. Here and around the coastline to the south of Sant Antoni is a vast 'prairie' of oceanic posidonia. This endemic Mediterranean plant, with roots, stalk, leaves and fruit, lives underwater to a depth of 40m (131ft). Posidonia contributes to coastal stability, protects beaches and is the habitat of numerous plant and animal species, some of which are threatened with extinction.

The Ses Salines Natural Park is also a bird sanctuary. The salt pans are one of the first ports of call for storks, herons and flamingos and other migrant species on their way to Africa, while permanent residents include black-necked grebes, warblers and ospreys. Theckla lark, blue rock thrush and crag martin can be found around the cliffs, while the outlying islands support colonies of gulls and cormorants. Sightings of the rare Eleanora's falcon, an endemic Balearic species, are not uncommon on Es Vedrà.

Ibiza's marine life is equally varied. The island's fishermen bring in regular trawls of tuna, amberjack, barracuda, scorpion fish, spiny lobster, grouper and John Dory while further out to sea one can expect to find turtles, hammerhead sharks and dolphins. Mention should also be made of the indigenous wall lizard *podarchis pityusensis*. This hardy reptile, bright green in colour and up to 7cm (3 inches) long, is easily spotted. Its natural habitat is barren, rocky land, but it can also be found near houses and around garden walls.

The environment
No one can pretend that the environment has not changed drastically in the Pitiusas over the last fifty years. Many people alive today can remember

the thick mantle of pine forest around Cala Llenya or the beach at Cala Vedella when there wasn't a building in sight.

It was the Committee for the Defence of the Salines, formed in 1977, which drew the proverbial line in the sand against untrammelled urban development. This initiative spawned a motley collection of environmental pressure groups, from GEN (Grup de Estudi de sa Naturalesa) to Friends of the Earth, which have been campaigning ever since. The aim was not just to stop the property developers, but to promote understanding of the ecology by encouraging islanders to restore disused fincas, wells and drystone walls and to

adopt traditional, environmentally friendly agricultural methods. These small-scale initiatives went hand in hand with the successful campaign to save Cala d'Hort which is one of the most valuable ecosystems in the Mediterranean (*see p14*). However, since the Popular Party and its conservative coalition partners were returned to power in the 2003 regional elections, the environmentalists have been on the defensive. Future campaigns will focus on the Ses Feixes marshes (*see p59*), doubling the width of the road from Eivissa to Sant Antoni and expanding the island's airport is planned at a cost of 72 million euros.

The windmill at Ses Salines

History

*c.*4500 BC	Earliest evidence of human settlement on the islands. Cave dwellers, originally from the Iberian peninsula.
*c.*1600 BC	Renewed Bronze Age settlement on Ibiza and Formentera.
*c.*800 BC	Evidence that the Talayotic peoples of Mallorca and Menorca are trading with Ibizan settlers.
*c.*700 BC	The Ancient Greeks explore the Ibizan coastline but never settle. They call the islands the *Pitiusas* on account of the proliferation of pine trees.
654 BC	The Carthaginians capture and colonise the islands. They name the island Ibosim, after the god Bes. The capital becomes one of the most important ports in the Mediterranean. Trade and commerce flourish.
1st century BC	Following an earlier source, the geographer, Diodorus Siculus, writes (correctly) that Ibiza is about the same size as the Greek island of Corfu.
146 BC	Carthage is destroyed by the Romans.
123 BC	Roman conquest of the Balearic islands. Ibosim is renamed Ebosus. In accordance with a pact, the islands are granted Confederate status. Coins are minted with the Emperor's image on one side and the figure of the Carthaginian god Bes on the other. Commerce expands with the export of salt and lead.
AD 70	The Roman Emperor Vespasian demotes Ebosus to a mere municipality within the empire.
421–5	The Vandals attack Ibiza and Formentera.
535	The Byzantine general, Belisarius, conquers the islands, which are incorporated into the eastern Empire.
693	Following the capture of Carthage by the Arabs, the islands are increasingly vulnerable to Moorish attack.
712	Ibiza and Formentera are incorporated into Visigothic Spain.

859	The islands are devastated by the Normans.
901–02	Ibiza and Formentera are conquered by the armies of the Emir of Córdoba and Islamicised, Ibiza being renamed Yebisah. The conquerors revolutionise agriculture, building irrigation ditches and planting rice, cotton and other crops. Olives and oranges are grown on hillside terraces which still exist today.
1114	The combined fleets of Pisa and Aragón descend on Ibiza with the blessing of the pope. Declaring a crusade, they take the citadel, lay the city waste and massacre the Muslim population but the islands remain under Arab control.
1235	On 12 August the armies of Guillem de Montgrí, Nuño Sans and the crown prince of Portugal conquer Yebisah, which becomes part of the kingdom of Catalunya. Formentera is annexed the following year. The islands are returned to Christianity, Catalan becomes the official language and the islanders are granted substantial privileges, including the right of self-government.

1261	A royal statute entitles the people of Ibiza to benefit directly from the profits of the salt industry.
1286	Ibiza and Formentera are formally annexed by the independent kingdom of Mallorca.
1299	A decree issued by Jaume II of Mallorca creates the Universitat, which becomes the municipal government of the islands. Ibiza is divided into four *quartons*: Santa Eulària, Sant Miquel de Balansat, Sant Antoni de Portmany and Sant Jordi.
1348	The Black Death reduces the population of Ibiza, to around 2,000. By 1400 Formentera is completely uninhabited.
1359	An attack on Ibiza by Pedro the Cruel is repulsed by Guillermo de Llagostera. Pedro el Ceremonioso subsequently repairs the walls of Dalt Vila.
1498	The Franciscans administer the new church of Nuestra Señora de Jesús, founded in the village of the same name.

1518	Spanish troops are billeted in Ibiza during Carlos I's offensive against Algeria. They sack the island after the government fails to pay them.
1554–5	Felipe II of Spain commissions the Roman military engineer, Giovanni Battista Calvi, to reconstruct the walls of Dalt Vila.
1584	Completion of the Ses Taules gateway sets the seal on the new Dalt Vila fortifications.
1587	The Dominicans receive permission to build a monastery within the walls of Dalt Vila.
1686	The Jesuits establish their first community on the islands.
1697	The repopulation of Formentera gets under way.
1708	The Dominicans found a free school in their monastery in Dalt Vila, Eivissa.
1767	The Jesuits are expelled from the islands.
1789	The Spanish monarchy commissions wholesale reforms on the islands. Public works programmes and modest improvements in health and education follow.
1800–15	Additional taxes, and the cost of the corsairs' allowances during the Napoleonic Wars and the Spanish War of Independence, imposes severe hardship on the people of the islands.
1846	A new periodical, *The Ibizan*, is produced on the island's first printing press.
1848	Eivissa begins to expand beyond Sa Marina with the founding of the *Poble Nou* (New Town).
1871	The Spanish government sells the salt pans of Ses Salines to a private company.
1875– 1900	Emigration to the United States, Cuba and South America intensifies, as many Ibizans, especially young males, find it impossible to make a living on the island.
1885– 1912	Construction of the new port in Eivissa harbour entails the closing of the straits between the islets of Grossa, Plana and Botafoc.

1892	Ibiza gets its own daily newspaper, the *Diario de Ibiza*.
1936–9	The Spanish Civil War. Ibiza falls to the Nationalists and is placed under the authority of a military governor, General Goded. People divide along Nationalist and Republican lines and there are massacres on both sides, as well as wholesale destruction of property. Franco's forces imprison Republicans in Dalt Vila and establish a concentration camp in La Savina, Formentera.
1950	The Balearic Islands receive 98,000 visitors annually.
1958	Ibiza Airport opens to commercial traffic. Plans are outlined for the remodelling of Sant Antoni de Portmany.
1960	During the following decade Ibiza is colonised by hippies.
1969	Eivissa is declared an Historic and Artistic Monument with protected status.
1970	The Balearic Islands now welcome around 400,000 visitors annually.
1975	Death of the dictator General Francisco Franco, ending more than forty years of autocratic government and the suppression of the Catalan culture.
1983	Estatut d'Autonomía (Decree of Autonomy) recognises the special historical, cultural and political identity of the Balearic people. Catalan becomes an official language on a par with Castilian (Spanish).
1986	Spain joins the European Economic Community (later the EU).
1999	Regional elections bring a progressive coalition to power which, three years later, introduces the controversial ecotax.
2003	The Conservatives are returned to power in new regional elections and the ecotax is abandoned. Ibiza and Formentera welcome nearly two million visitors a year, while 85 per cent of the population of the Balearic Islands earns a living, directly or indirectly, from the tourist industry.

Governance

The regional elections of May 2003 proved disastrous for the *Pacte Progresista*, the coalition of Socialist and Greens which had governed the Balearic Islands for the previous four years. The triumph of the right – no surprise in itself, as Conservative forces have dominated local politics for more than two decades – has been seen as a victory for the developers over the environmentalists, presaged by the scrapping of the controversial ecotax.

Dalt Vila town hall is in a former Dominican convent

The ecotax

The programme of the *Pacte Progresista* had a bold ecological thrust, with proposals to halt the rampant advance of urban development, prevent further deforestation, improve the management of water and other scarce resources, ring-fence areas of natural beauty for special protection, and encourage visitors to respect the environment. There was a general feeling that 'enough was enough', that, despite the huge economic benefits of tourism, the interest of the islands' 800,000 residents had not been well-served by the holiday industry and its ten million clients, and that the region had already suffered huge, possibly irreversible, environmental damage. The ecotax was intended to make tourism more sustainable by funding a steady flow of improvements – from bulldozing eyesore hotels to creating a visitors' centre in the Ses Salines Natural Park. It was anticipated that the levy of up to two euros a day on the cost of hotel accommodation would generate an income of more than 60 million euros annually. From the outset there was

fierce resistance from the property developers and hoteliers and from tour operators fearful of a further drop in bookings in the aftermath of the September 11 tragedy in the USA. The Spanish Government, led by the centre-right Popular Party, challenged the tax in the courts and it was only introduced (in May 2002) after the constitutional court lifted an injunction.

Cala d'Hort

The environmental lobby enjoyed one notable success in Ibiza, the creation of the Cala d'Hort Natural Park. A proposal in 1992 to build a golf course in this area of outstanding natural beauty provoked an angry response, and a makeshift coalition of pressure groups, including *Amics de la Terra* (Friends of the Earth) and the *Grup d'Estudi de la Naturalesa* (GEN), was formed to fight the proposal. The campaign lasted for more than seven years and culminated in an unprecedented demonstration by 12,000 banner-carrying protesters through the streets of Eivissa. When the *Pacte Progresista* came to power, work on

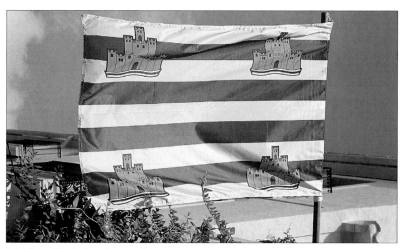

Dalt Vila emblazoned on the town flag

the golf course was halted and, two years later, Cala d'Hort was given special protected status.

Autonomy

Since 1983, the Balearic Islands have enjoyed a large measure of self-government as one of Spain's *comunidades autónomas*. The *Govern de Las Islas Balears* is made up of three *Consells Insulars* (Mallorca, Menorca and Ibiza-Formentera) and a democratically elected parliament with tax-raising and legislative functions. The parliament also nominates a president (since 2003, the Popular Party's Jaume Matas). Foreign residents have been able to vote in regional elections since 1994. Whatever their differences, most politicians see eye to eye on the vigorous promotion of the historical, cultural and political identity of the region, denied to it for decades by General Franco. Central to this is the dissemination of the Catalan language in the press, on TV and in schools and offices.

CORRUPTION

There have been a number of corruption scandals in recent years involving Spanish politicians and property developers. While the most prominent cases have occurred on the mainland, in September 2003 the *Caso Formentera* was finally brought before the judges of the Balearic High Court. This case dates back to the regional elections of 1999 when a Popular Party candidate, Carlos Gutiérrez, was accused of purloining postal votes from Argentina. What really set hackles rising, however, was his subsequent appointment as a senator by Balearic president Jaume Matas while the case was still *sub judice*. Several other members of Matas' previous administration are facing allegations of embezzlement and misappropriation of funds.

On 8 August 1235 the forces of Jaume I of Aragón and Catalunya, under the command of Guillem de Montgrí, archbishop of Tarragona, captured the citadel of Yebisah after a short siege, so ending more than four centuries of Arab rule. Tradition has it that the invaders entered through a secret tunnel following a tip-off from the governor's brother – the pair had fallen out over a woman. Whatever the truth of the story, the Catalan invasion changed the course of Mediterranean history.

Golden age

The crown of Aragón imposed its own laws and institutions, insisted on the use of the Catalan language and restored the Catholic religion. But the conquerors were generous in victory. By the *Carta de Franquicias* the islanders gained a measure of self-government, an independent judiciary, tax exemptions and the abolition of conscription. They were also allowed to exploit the highly lucrative salt industry. The Pitiusas were now under the protection of a powerful mercantile state with possessions scattered throughout the Mediterranean. The population increased as settlers from the mainland were encouraged to colonise the islands. The capital – renamed Eivissa – prospered and was given its own administration, the *Universitat*, but at

the expense of the countryside which rapidly became impoverished. Ibiza was already in decline when the Spanish abolished the Catalan administration following the War of the Spanish Succession (1702–14).

Revival

At the time of Franco's death in 1975, the survival of Catalan culture was in the balance. For the previous forty years, the Fascist regime had suppressed every expression of regionalism in Spain. The Catalan language was confined to the home. Newspaper, radio and TV output was exclusively in Castilian (Spanish) and Catalan was outlawed in offices and schools. In 1983, the new regional government set about reversing the trend, but it was no easy task. Ironically, the decade following the end of Franco's rule saw the proportion of Catalan speakers fall. The tourist boom of the 1960s had fuelled a population increase of more than 40 per cent as migrants from the poorer regions of southern Spain and North Africa came looking for work. Fear that Catalan culture might be 'swamped' by outsiders has led to a vigorous, at times aggressive, promotion of the language, for example a recent decree obliging teachers and public servants to speak Catalan. This in turn has led to resentment and some outright opposition. At the local level, a petition protesting the introduction of Catalan street names in the small community of Jesús in Ibiza collected more than 300 signatures. Significantly, the opponents of the scheme, mainly wealthy residents from the mainland, succeeded in having the scheme overturned. Yet, when all is said and done, Catalan, though a minority language, is spoken by around ten million people, from Catalunya and the Balearic Islands to Sardinia and the Pyrenees – more speakers in fact than Danish and Norwegian.

Opposite: Local and Catalan flags fly on Ibizan public buildings
Above: A Catalan sign welcoming visitors to Santa Eulària

Culture

Visitors who notice something familiar about the whitewashed, cuboid houses of the Ibizan countryside are not mistaken. Functional, minimalist in form and in perfect harmony with the landscape, the humble *casament* influenced the development of two important schools of 20th-century architecture, the Bauhaus and the Modern Movement. Erwin Broner and Josep Lluís Sert, both disciples of Le Corbusier, did more than anyone to promote the *estilo ibicenco*, both internationally and on the island.

Castanyoles (castanets) are larger and louder than their Spanish cousins

Domestic architecture

The *casament* (described by Sert as 'the timeless root of a house both rational and full of sculptural force') is arguably the most enduring legacy of the Arabs to the peoples of the Pitiusas. A key component are the metre-thick double walls, the intervening space filled with rubble and mortar which hardens like adobe. Designed to regulate the temperature, these walls are remarkably successful in retaining the heat in winter

Whitewashed houses dotted around the landscape of Sant Carles

and holding it at bay during the long hot summers. The same logic dictates the number of openings – kept to a minimum, but strategically placed to let in the maximum amount of light. The roof is flat and waterproofed with charcoal, while precious rainwater is collected in tiled gutters on either side. Inside, the rooms are arranged around a large central space, the *porxo*, where the extended family gathered at mealtimes or for weddings and other celebrations. The bedrooms, living quarters, stables and storerooms are all under the one roof. If more space is required, the modular form allows any number of identical units to be built on to the main structure. Outside is the *porchada*, a canopied porch cool enough for the afternoon siesta or even for sleeping through the sultry nights of July and August. Other elements of the *casament* are the *pozo* (well), usually sited close to the porch, and a small garden for growing herbs and vegetables.

Where to see traditional houses: The best examples are in the Els Amunts Natural Park in the north of the island, especially around Sant Vicent de sa Cala. Otherwise, visit the Ethnology Museum in Santa Eulària which is actually

Ethnology Museum, Santa Eulària

A male dancer impressing his female partner

Music and dance

The traditional ceremonial dance, the *ball-pagès*, is rooted in courtship ritual, though its origins are more primitive. Anthropologists have noted pronounced similarities with a war dance introduced to Russia by the cossacks but originating in Kurdistan. The protagonists of the Ibizan folk dance, male and female, each has an assigned role. The woman, though far from passive, is always submissive, never looking her partner directly in the eye. The male, on the other hand, struts about like a cockerel – the symbolism is deliberate – eschewing specific steps in favour of wild leaps and bounds. Following a

located in a *casament*. There are numerous instances of modern houses influenced by the traditional Ibizan style, for example *Carrer de Sa Bomba 18, Sa Penya (Eivissa)* – the work of Le Corbusier, no less.

Festeig

The traditional courting ritual (*festeig*) was observed until comparatively recent times and took place in the *porchada*. A girl of marriageable age would leave the house, dressed in her finest clothes and chaperoned by her father, to meet prospective suitors. Like the princes in a fairy tale, each would approach her in a predetermined order and do his best to win her over. This was a leisurely ritual that might continue over several consecutive afternoons. The community would know that the girl had made up her mind when she appeared at mass, wearing a ring on every finger but not the thumb.

CATALAN LANGUAGE

A Romance language with roots in mediaeval Latin and Provençal French, Catalan was fully formed by the end of the 11th century, the first written texts appearing shortly afterwards. In Ibiza and Formentera the dialect is known as *Eivissenc*. This preserves some of the Balearic vocabulary already outmoded in Catalonia itself, most obviously the old definite articles es, sa and ses for el, la and les, which are commonly used in place names. *Eivissenc* also incorporates some words from the Valencian dialect of Catalan as well as some indigenous words, such as *major* instead of *avi* (granddad).

signal on the castanets, the dance begins at a slow tempo with the *curta* (literally, 'short'). The female waits on her partner, who approaches in a swaggering, extrovert manner. She responds by tracing figures of eight on the ground, moving her body in time with the music. The tempo now accelerates, heralding the second part of the dance, known as the *llarga* (long). Provoked by the woman's modesty, the male is emboldened, his body language suggesting more than a touch of arrogance. The female makes ever-widening circles around him until, driven to the point of distraction, he reaches her with a single spectacular jump, only to crown her with his hands before kneeling submissively at her feet. The musical accompaniment is provided by a small ensemble of folk instruments: the *castanyoles* (castanets), larger (and louder) than the Spanish equivalent; a single flute, traditionally made from oleander and encrusted with metal; the

reclam de xeremies, a double reed instrument belonging to the clarinet family, and the *tambor*, a decorated drum made from pine wood.

Costume

The elegance of the *traje blanco*, the traditional folk dress worn by women in summer, inspired the Ad Lib fashion designers of the 1970s. The essential element is a white blouse and flounced, multilayered skirt, invented, so it is said, to convince marauding pirates that the wearer was pregnant. In winter, Ibizan women change into the *gonella*, a pleated, black woollen tunic with buttoned sleeves, worn under a delicately embroidered bodice. A linen shawl is drawn over the shoulders and fastened at the chest, while fibre espadrilles and a broad-brimmed hat, decorated with flowers, complete the ensemble. The most important ornament is the *emprendada*, a tiered necklace of silver, gold and coral, with an elaborate jewelled cross at the centre. The male costume is more straightforward: white linen shirt with ruffled, stand-up collar, white trousers, red sash, black waistcoat and red, tasselled beret.

Where to see traditional folk dancing: Folk troupes perform at the annual patronal festivals of all major villages in Ibiza and Formentera. In addition, the groups Colla de Vila and Colla de Sa Bodega perform every Friday throughout the summer in the cloister of Dalt Vila town hall, Eivissa, starting at 9.30pm.

Showing off the *emprendada* necklace

Festivals and Events

Three annual celebrations – the pre-Lenten Carnaval, Easter and Corpus Christi – vary in date as they are religious festivals. Carnaval (*see below*) also depends on the fall of Lent. Corpus Christi falls seven weeks after Easter.

Colourful folk display in Eivissa town hall

Each community in Ibiza and Formentera has its *dia patronal* or patron saint's day. On these colourful occasions everyone lets their hair down and villagers wear the traditional folk costume, including the *emprendada*, the collar handed down from mother to daughter (*see p21*).

Village saints' days include:
12 February – Santa Eulària
19 March – Sant Josep
5 April – Sant Vicent
25 July – Sant Jaume (Formentera)
4 November – Sant Carles
16 November – Santa Gertrudis

Cap d'Any
1 January
In the capital, New Year celebrations centre on Plaça Vara del Rey. Revellers swallow twelve grapes, one for each stroke of midnight.

Cabalgata del Reyes
5 January, Eivissa and other main towns
Procession of the Three Kings on the eve of the day when Spanish children traditionally receive their Christmas presents.

Festa Patronal de Sant Antoni de Portmany
16–17 January
Blessing of pets and other animals on Passeig des Fonts. Local delicacies, including sausages, are grilled on bonfires.

Carnaval
Fancy-dress parades and mischief, including the gentle ribbing of local public figures.

Semana Santa
Week before Easter
On the last three days of Holy Week images of Jesus and the Virgin are carried through the streets in solemn procession. The most impressive events take place in Eivissa and Santa Eulària on Good Friday.

Feria Nautica
Mid-April, Santa Eulària
Boat fair in the marina.

Anar a Maig
First Sunday in May, Santa Eulària
Procession of horse-drawn carts bedecked with flowers. Firework display and folklore festival. The local agricultural and motor fairs are also held at this time.

Eivissa Medieval
Second weekend in May (see p152)

Moda Ad Lib
End of May, Eivissa
Fashion parades attract Spanish TV celebrities and people from the show business world.

Corpus Christi
June, Eivissa
The host is carried in procession from the Cathedral to the church of St Elm, honouring a tradition dating back to the 14th century.

Focs de la Nit de Sant Joan
23–24 June
Huge bonfires are lit to mark St John's Eve, the shortest night of the year. In Eivissa, celebrations focus on Plaça Enrique Fajarnes.

Jazz Festival
First two weeks in July: Dalt Vila, Eivissa
Concerts showcase young musical talent.

Dia de Verge de Carmen
16 July, coastal towns and villages, especially Eivissa, Sant Antoni and Es Cubells (Ibiza) and La Savina (Formentera)
Feast day of the patroness of seafarers.

Statues of the virgin are carried to the harbour where fishing boats, lit by Chinese lanterns and festooned with streamers and pennants, are blessed by a priest.

Festas Patronales
5, 8 August, Eivissa (see pp152–3)

Dia de Sant Bartolomeu
24 August, Sant Antoni
Firework display in the harbour with swimming races, slingshot competitions and folk concerts.
Sant Agusti
The married men of the village challenge the bachelors to a football match.

Festa Patronal de Sant Miquel de Balansat
29 September
Village fair. Pigs are slaughtered and consumed as *butifarrò* (black pudding) and other delicacies.

Festa Pagesa
Sunday following 15 October, Es Cubells
Country dancing performed by troupes from around the island.

Festa Patronal de Sant Francesc, Formentera
3 December
Bonfire outside the church, followed by a roast pork feast.

Nadal
6 December – 5 January, Eivissa
Christmas fair on Vara de Rey.
24 December, across the islands
Churches are decorated with flowers for candlelit midnight mass.

Palm Sunday procession

Ibiza receives around 1,850,000 foreign visitors a year, mainly from Britain (35 per cent) and Germany (30 per cent). Compare this with a figure of 98,000 for the entire Balearic region in 1950 and the scale of the influx becomes apparent. Tourism has had a profound impact, not least on the island's economy. Traditionally an agricultural society, today more than four out of five islanders depend on tourism, directly or indirectly, for their survival.

When the number of visitors fell by around ten per cent in 2002, the first drop in more than a decade, alarm bells started to ring. Hoteliers, property developers, shopkeepers, politicians, the man and woman in the street poured over the statistics and began analysing possible reasons for the downturn. All kinds of suggestions were put forward – the terrorist attack on New York on September 11, cut-price holidays on the Turkish coast, the crisis in the German economy, the ecotax – there was even a heated debate over whether the island would receive more visitors if the travel brochures were to refer to it as Eivissa rather than Ibiza. In fact, things were not as black as they seemed. 'Quality' tourism, for example, remained largely unaffected, with the yachting industry reporting 'business as usual' and the increasingly important gay market equally untroubled. However, it is true that tourists, Germans especially, are spending considerably less than they were a decade ago. Resorts like Sant Antoni have become over-dependent on package holidays and mass tourism (the sector hardest hit by the recession), with clients tending to opt for shorter stays. Ibiza continues to rely heavily on the youth market, a loyal constituency up to now, but a demanding one, constantly on the lookout for something new or different. The clubbing scene, one of the island's most important sources of tourist revenue, remains popular with the Brits and now has a wider European following. Celebrity appearances by the likes of Kylie Minogue, Sting and Puff Daddy have helped keep Pacha,

El Divino and the rest in the public eye. That said, the tourist industry will have to broaden its base – attracting families and Third Age visitors, and developing a winter season – something Mallorca has been doing successfully for years. In other words, Ibiza's image may well have to change.

The coffee tables of hotel lounges across the island are littered with glossy brochures offering a bewildering variety of properties for sale. Succumb to temptation and you will be joining the 13,000 foreign residents (mainly British and German) who have already set up home here. This represents a little more than 13 per cent of the total population and numbers are set to rise. In fact, native Ibizans now account for less than 50 per cent of islanders, the remainder comprising migrants from the Spanish mainland and seasonal workers from Ecuador and Morocco who are employed in the construction and service industries. It is a moot point

whether Ibiza is on its way to losing its traditional culture and identity, even its voice. Since 1994 foreign residents have been entitled to vote in municipal elections. So far, relatively few have exercised this right but the signs are that attitudes may be changing. Regional politicians are increasingly sensitive to the needs of foreign constituents who might one day sweep them from office.

Opposite page: Late night shopping in Dalt Vila
Above: Ibiza is home to a thriving community of commercial artists
Left: Watching the sunset, Café del Mar, Sant Antoni

Impressions

With three hundred days of sunshine a year and four hours a day even in January, Ibiza is an all-year holiday spot. The hottest period, from June to late September, is also the busiest, when hotel prices, car rental charges and club tickets peak and the population increases tenfold.

Statue in Plaça des Parc, Eivissa

When to go

If you are holidaying in July and August, try to do your sightseeing in the mornings (the earlier the better) and then spend the afternoon lingering over lunch or taking a nap. Remember that shops and boutiques stay open until midnight, so you can buy gifts and souvenirs in the cool of the evening.

Out of season, Ibiza is almost unrecognisable. The beaches are empty and the roads infinitely less crowded. Arrive early in the autumn and you will be able to take advantage of the end-of-season sales in the shops and boutiques. In spring the flowers are in bloom and

View across the stunning bay of Cala de Sant Vicent

Tour buses explore Ibiza's captivating interior

the countryside, freshened by spring rains, is ravishing. Winters are mild with little rainfall, although sudden downpours and occasional storms can be expected. Swimming is possible from May to November and even beyond, although only the hardiest souls take the plunge in February. Travel out of season and you will also get to meet the islanders and perhaps practise your Spanish and Catalan.

What to wear

During July and August, women will be more comfortable in skirts and dresses than trousers, while shorts and T-shirt are *de rigueur* for men. Cotton trousers are less 'clingy' than jeans, and sandals are preferable to trainers and sports shoes. (When exposing your feet, remember to protect them with sun block and mosquito spray.) Some form of head covering is essential to avoid overexposure to the sun. There are no dress codes, except in the most exclusive hotels and restaurants. For most of the year, the air is warm enough to sit out of doors in only a light jumper. From mid-September, however, you may need a jumper or light jacket in the evenings, and a waterproof, just to be on the safe side.

Information

The best tourist office is in Eivissa (Passeig des Moll). The staff are friendly and helpful and have a good command of foreign languages. The offices in Santa Eulària, Sant Antoni and La Savina (Formentera) are equally obliging, but brochures and leaflets tend to be more localised. All offices supply lists of accommodation, bars and restaurants, town plans (including an excellent map of Dalt Vila), bus timetables etc. They will also have information on organised excursions (ask about EcoEivissa, tel: (971) 30 23 47). The Eivissa branch offers free tours of Dalt Vila, the Punic sites at Puig des Molins and Cala d'Hort and the Phoenician settlement at Sa Caleta. Similar excursions are available on Formentera.

Lingering over lunch in Plaça des Parc

Catalan) – it is good for morale and will earn you Brownie points from locals. Try to adapt to the Spanish way of life: choose a restaurant that serves local or Spanish dishes, enjoy a leisurely lunch, then take a short snooze – a recent survey confirmed what the locals have always believed, that a daily 30-minute siesta is good for you.

On the beach

Most large beaches have red-cross stations and lifeguards, and buoys mark the areas safest for swimming. Hidden rocks can be treacherous, especially in the smaller coves along the north coast. There are two official nudist beaches, at Es Cavallet (favoured by gay tourists) and Aigües Blanques. Topless bathing is acceptable almost anywhere. Beach umbrellas are available for hire in the resorts, but you will need to bring your own to the more isolated coves. The one essential item is a high-factor sun block. Bring plenty, reapply after swimming ('water resistant' is a misleading term), and cover *all* exposed areas, including the tops and soles of feet. Avoid sunbathing between noon and 5pm when the sun is at its hottest, and beware of dozing off on the sand or at the poolside. One dose of sunburn can ruin a holiday. Consuming iced drinks when exposed to the sun can produce gippy tummy and dizziness, so

Going local

There are certain times of the year in Ibiza when you may hear yourself asking the question: 'Am I in Spain?' German and English seem more common than Catalan, and every other bar and restaurant offers fish and chips, Sunday roasts and Sky sports. To enjoy the authentic Ibiza (Formentera presents less of a problem in this respect), spend more time inland or in the smaller coastal settlements. Pick up a smattering of one of the local languages (Spanish or

The water at inviting Platja de Talamanca

save them for the terrace. Beach restaurants and *chiringuitos* (snack shacks) are usually closed from the end of September to at least the beginning of May. One final word of warning: bring only the cash you are likely to need, and never leave bags unattended – thieves never take a holiday.

Getting around

Eivissa airport is at Ses Salines, about 7km (4 miles) from the town. The taxi fare is reasonable, though you will save money by taking the bus (hourly service from early morning until 10.35pm).

Buses: Connections between the main towns – Eivissa, Sant Antoni and Santa Eulària – are excellent, though at peak times buses are crowded and you may have to stand. There are regular services to Sant Miquel and Portinatx on the north coast and to some popular beaches – Es Canar, Port d'Es Torrent and Ses Salines, for example. Other destinations are less easily accessed. Buses also operate on Formentera.

Ferries: Boats ply the coastline around the three main resorts and are a pleasant and leisurely way of getting about. Most excursions include a swimming stop. Tickets are sold from kiosks on the waterfront, usually about one hour before departure. Demand is high, so do not leave buying until the last minute. In season, there are regular shuttle services to nearby beaches (Ses Salines, Port d'Es Torrent, Es Canar). Excursions are also available on Formentera (*see p122*).

Taxis are relatively inexpensive. There are no meters – prices are fixed according to the destination. Rates are posted outside the main taxi ranks and are available from tourist offices – alternatively, consult the driver beforehand. The round-the-island excursion is useful for a quick orientation. Taxis are white with a coloured diagonal stripe across the front door. A green light signals that the taxi is for hire.

Cycling: This is by far the most enjoyable way of getting around Formentera and presents few problems even for the athletically challenged – most of the terrain is relatively flat. There are numerous bike-hire firms on the quayside at La Savina – hire a mountain bike if you intend travelling to the far end of the island which involves an uphill climb. Cycling is also possible on Ibiza, but here the gradients are steeper and you'll need to be fit. There are only a few rental agencies – ask at the tourist office for details. For ideas on where to cycle, pick up a copy of *Rutes Cicloturisme*. These routes outline itineraries of between 24km (15 miles) and 56km (35 miles), indicating gradients, and should be used in conjunction with a more detailed map.

Hiking: The series *Rutas des Falcó* (also available from the tourist office) sets out walks of varying levels of difficulty, all of which are signposted. When out walking, wear comfortable shoes or boots with a good grip. Take a detailed map as insurance against getting lost. Break yourself in gently, allow plenty of time and never set out in bad weather. Bring food, plenty of water, and sun block. Always wear a head covering of some description and do not forget your binoculars!

Driving: Ibiza has a good, fairly comprehensive road network. Surfaces are in an excellent state of repair (better, in fact, than many on the mainland), but a four-wheel-drive vehicle may be necessary to negotiate the dirt tracks leading to the more remote coves and beaches. Lack of rain during the summer can mean slippery surfaces – a

particular hazard for two-wheel-drive vehicles. There are petrol stations in main towns and settlements but fewer along the roadside, so fill the tank before setting out. Spanish drivers are inclined to take risks, so avoid the temptation to imitate them. Observe speed limits and remember that many coastal roads have challenging hairpin bends. The sign *Ceda el paso* at junctions and crossroads means 'give way to the right'. Avoid driving at night, as roads are poorly lit and some clubbers will inevitably be under the influence of drink or drugs.

Bicycles resting at Platja Llevant, Trucador Peninsula

Eivissa

Known in Spanish as Pueblo Ibiza (Ibiza Town), the capital of the Pitiusas (population 31,500) is a major tourist attraction, with enough to interest visitors for at least a couple of days. The fortress city of Dalt Vila is on UNESCO's World Heritage list and would rate five stars by any standard. Allow at least half a day to see it. Then there are the quaint fishermen's quarters below the walls and the port with its marinas, restaurants and nightclubs. Add to that the best-conserved Punic burial site in the Mediterranean and at least three beaches within a radius of 4km (2.5 miles) and you have all the ingredients for an enjoyable stay.

View to the Cathedral, Dalt Vila

Eivissa is the ideal base for touring the island. Communications with Santa Eulària, Sant Antoni and the north of the island are excellent and there are regular daily sailings to Formentera.

Dalt Vila

When Dalt Vila was declared a World Heritage Site in 1999, its almost perfectly preserved Renaissance fortifications were judged to be of

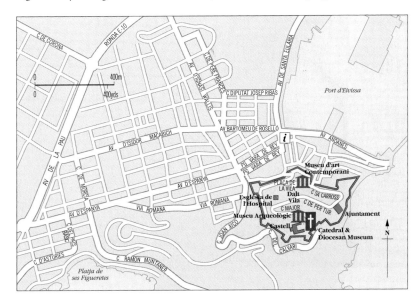

'singular historic, architectural and cultural value.' The sights of the 'Upper Town' include the walls and bastions, the cathedral, the castle, a 16th-century monastery (now the town hall), several museums, some splendid mansions dating from the 15th to the 19th centuries, and a number of picturesque squares thoughtfully provided with café terraces, restaurants and gift shops. From almost any point along the walls there are breathtaking views of Eivissa town and bay, the beaches of Figueretes and d'en Bossa, the salt marshes of Ses Salines and the island of Formentera.

Ajuntament (Town hall)

This 16th-century building was originally a Dominican monastery. The first monks arrived on the island around 1580 and made their headquarters in the parish church at Jesús. A pirate raid prompted second thoughts, and in 1587 they sought the protection of Dalt Vila's newly completed fortress walls. Here they remained until the disentailment of the monasteries in 1835 when the town councillors sent them packing and used the building as a prison, hospital and school, before moving in themselves. The arcaded cloister – all that remains of the original monastery – makes an attractive backdrop for the concerts of classical music and folk dancing displays held here from time to time. Next door to the town hall is the former monastic church, dedicated to **Sant Pere**, although the parishioners stubbornly insist on calling it Santo Domingo – it is the image of this saint which presides over the high altar. The church dates from 1592, although it was later given a pretty comprehensive Baroque facelift. The red-tiled domes and most of the interior decoration, including the ceiling frescos and Valencian *azulejos*, are from the later period. Outside the church, Carrer Balansat leads to the **Baluard de Santa Llúcia** and wonderful harbour views. The bastion, sometimes used for concerts, including a mini-jazz festival in July, is currently closed for restoration. It originally contained a gunpowder store, known as **Es Polvorí**, which blew up in 1730 after being struck by lightning, seriously damaging the Dominican convent nearby.

Església de Sant Pere. Open only during services (Sat 7pm, Sun 12am & 7pm).

Steps on Conquista, Dalt Vila

In the mid-16th century the greatest menace to Christian civilisation and the security of Europe was the Turk. Ottoman armies had already invaded the Balkans and would eventually reach the gates of Vienna. At sea, the reach of the Turkish navy extended from the Aegean to the north coast of Africa, from where its Berber allies launched crippling raids against Christian outposts in the Mediterranean, not least Ibiza. In 1554 the Hapsburg emperor Charles V decided that strengthening Dalt Vila's defences was a matter of urgency but it was his son and heir, Felipe II, who was to assume responsibility for the task.

The fortifications built by the Carthaginians around the 4th century BC, if not quite one of the wonders of the ancient world, had won the admiration of contemporaries and, in 217 BC, the walls withstood a siege by the Roman general Cornelius Scipio. Following the Arab conquest of the Pitiusas, the defences were extended to encompass the growing city. The walls were rebuilt on three successive levels and surmounted by a keep, the Almudaina. Although these fortifications were crumbling by the 16th century, it made sense to use them as the foundation for the new defences. Finding the money was the problem. The Spanish monarchy was strapped for cash and Felipe had to turn to the archbishop of Valencia, Tomás de Villanueva, for the initial down payment of 20,000 ducats. When costs spiralled by more than 150 per cent, the Spaniards raided the salt revenues. The military engineer hand-picked by the

king for the task was a Roman, Giovanni Battista Calvi. Calvi had an impressive track record, including the fortifications at Maó (Menorca), Palma (Mallorca) and Barcelona. His remit in Ibiza extended to the protection of Santa Eulària and the salt pans at Ses Salines. Calvi was assisted by four local master masons, Antoni Jaume, Gaspar Puig, Pere Francesc and Antoni Lobo. They began by constructing six massive pentagonal bastions (*baluardes*), later named Sant Joan, Santa Tecla, Sant Bernat, Sant Jordi, Sant Jaume and Portal Nou. Each was strategically positioned to guard part of the city and given its own garrison. The Berbers had increased their fire power over the years, so each bulwark was cleverly angled to deflect enemy fire. When the need arose, artillery pieces could be moved from one bastion to another along what is now known as Calvi's ring road (Ronda de Calvi). Work was already well advanced when, in 1575, another Italian engineer, Giovanni Paleazzo Fratin, was brought in to construct an extra bastion to guard the Vila Nova, the 'new town' of Santa Llúcia, after which the corresponding bulwark was named. By 1585 the defences were complete. Dalt Vila was girdled by walls 5m (16.5ft) thick, 25m (20.5ft) high and 2km (1.25 miles) in length. There is a note of defiance, disdain even, in the elegance of Calvi's design – a confidence bordering on certainty that the defences would never be breached. And they never were. Eivissa was rid of the pirate menace for good.

Opposite: Calvi's walls have stood the test of time
Above: Cannon could be wheeled from one bastion to another via Calvi's 'ring road'

Capella de Sant Ciriac

Candles burn before the small shrine dedicated to Sant Ciriac, whose patronal feast falls on 8 August, the anniversary of the Catalan invasion in 1235. Peer in, and behind the grill you should be able to make out the entrance to a sealed-up tunnel. It was through this passageway that the first of Guillem de Montgrí's forces penetrated the Arab defences – after receiving a tip-off, so the story goes, from the governor's treacherous brother. (They had fallen out over a girl in the harem.) The chapel, completed in 1752, is the focus of an annual service of commemoration when flowers are laid before the image of the saint.

Carrer Major

Dalt Vila's main street is lined with handsome mansions built by the cream of the Catalan aristocracy. Or so they claimed when they arrived in Ibiza, later advertising their lineage by carving spurious but highly imaginative coats of arms into the façades. **Can Llaudis**, at No 18, is rated the finest example of civilian Catalan Gothic architecture on the island. Built around an interior courtyard, a Renaissance staircase leads to what were the living quarters on the main floor. Note the crest of the Laudes family, who owned the house before it passed into the hands of the Comasemas, a merchant family from Mallorca, in the 18th century. Can Llaudis used to house a collection of paintings by the distinguished Ibizan artist, Narcís Puget Viñas (1874–1960). Unfortunately, the humidity damaged the works, which are now being restored in the Archaeological Museum. Can

18th-century shrine honouring Sant Ciriac

Balansat (No 10) was the ancestral home of one of Ibiza's most distinguished families – note the 16th-century windows. **Torre del Canónigo** (No 8), now a hotel, is built on mediaeval foundations which conceal an Arab cistern.

Carrer Per Tur

Retired corsairs who had made their fortune defending Ibiza's honour on the high seas were among the owners of the mansions which grace this street. Look out particularly for **Can Montero** (No 1), a 17th-century building originally owned by a Genoese family of merchants. **Can Mariano Tur** (No 3) dates from the 18th century, **Can Llobet** (No 7) from the 19th century and **Casa Verdera** (No 6) from the 17th century. Just at the end of Carrer de Per Tur, on Carrer Joan Roman (No 2), is the **Antic Seminari**, which the Jesuits made their headquarters from 1669 until the order was expelled from Spain in 1767. This 'des res' has been converted into luxury apartments.

Castell

The castle guards the summit of Dalt Vila, occupying the rock on which the city was founded more than 2,600 years ago. Excavations beneath the site have yielded the remains of dwellings from the Punic period, and wells from the time of the Moorish occupation. The present castle incorporates what remains of the Arab fortress known as the *Almudaina* where the governor of Yebisah resided. The buildings have been remodelled on a number of occasions, most recently in the 18th century when the castle was used as a barracks. An access staircase was added in 1993, though the castle is still closed to the public. A controversial proposal for a car park, gift shop, café and luxury hotel on the site appears to have been scrapped, but there are plans to open at least some of the rooms.
Closed for restoration.

Close up view of Dalt Vila castle

Eye-catching tiled roof of the Dominican convent, Dalt Vila

Catedral

Before setting out on their historic mission to conquer Ibiza, Guillem de Montgrí and his followers made a solemn vow that, should they be successful, they would build a church dedicated to the Virgin. 'Our Lady of the Snows' may not be the most obvious patroness for a sunny island but her feast day occurs on 5 August, conveniently close to the anniversary of the invasion. This site has been a place of worship since the city was founded. The Carthaginians built a temple to the god Eshmun here in the 7th century. The Romans followed suit and, when the Moors arrived, they built a mosque over the ruins, which the Catalans consecrated for Christian worship. Work on the new cathedral began early in the 14th century but dragged on for over 200 years. The project was financed, in part at least, by profits from the lucrative salt trade. Only the side chapels, the sacristy and the bell tower are in the Catalan Gothic style. The rest of the building was given an insensitive makeover in the 18th century by a group of Valencian architects, including Pere Ferrer who built the parish church in Sant Josep (*see p106*). The best of the artwork, including 15th-century paintings by Francesc Gomes and a retable attributed to Valentí Montiliu, may eventually find its way to the Diocesan Museum (*see below*).
Cathedral. Open: daily 10am–1pm, but not for visits during Sunday mass 10.30am. Free.

The cathedral bell tower is a Dalt Vila landmark

Diocesan Museum

Also known as the Museo de la Catedral, this is due to reopen shortly in the sacristy and chapter house of the cathedral. The collection comprises all kinds of sacral art, from religious paintings

The Museum of Modern Art was founded in the 1960s

and enamels to jewel-encrusted vestments and gleaming gold and silver plate. One of the museum's prize possessions is a monstrance made in Mallorca in the late 14th or early 15th century.
Closed for restoration.

Església de l'Hospital

Near the old seminary (*see p106*) on the corner of Sant Josep and Santa Fac is the plain, whitewashed façade of a 15th-century hospital for the poor. The church dates from 1423 and was the focal point of the small community who lived here – a special viewing balcony was built so that the sick patients could see the priest saying mass. This was also the seat of the Confraternity of the Blood, a lay brotherhood, whose duties included accompanying condemned prisoners to the scaffold. The Església de

l'Hospital is now a cultural centre and is occasionally used for art exhibitions.

Museu d'Art Contemporani

The Contemporary Art Museum is housed in the Baluard de Sant Joan, immediately to the right of Portal de Ses Taules. It was originally used as an arsenal and armoury. The museum was founded in 1966 when artists from as far afield as the United States and Japan, as well as Western Europe, formed a close community on the island, seduced by the landscape and the bohemian lifestyle in equal measure. Their work is now on display here, alongside that of Ibizan and Spanish contemporaries. Keep an eye out for temporary exhibitions.
Open: May–Sept, Tue–Fri 10am–1.30pm, 5–8pm, Sat 10am–1.30pm; Oct–Apr, Tue–Fri 10am–1pm, 4–6pm, Sat 10am–1.30pm. Admission charge.

Museu Arqueològic d'Eivissa I Formentera

The archaeological museum has a modest but interesting collection of prehistoric, Phoenician, Roman and Islamic artefacts, spanning nearly 3,000 years of Ibizan history. The big disappointment is the Punic collection, most of which is now in the sister museum at the Puig des Molins site, closed indefinitely for restoration. The displays are arranged chronologically in half a dozen well-lit rooms. All the items are clearly labelled in English as well as Spanish. The finds, from excavations across the Pitiusas, include Prehistoric bone tools and axe heads, pottery and ceramics, jewellery, glassware, coins and statuary. The period of the Phoenician colonisation is well represented, with perfume bottles from Italy, Egyptian scarabs and Spanish amphorae, reflecting the wide commercial and cultural reach of this great seafaring people. Look out for the originals of the statues guarding Ses Taules, Roman coins with the image of the Emperor on one side and the Punic goddess Tanit (Bes) on the other, and some of the earthenware figures of Tanit discovered in the sanctuary at Es Cuieram. The museum occupies a number of buildings of historical importance. At the core is the 15th-century headquarters of the Universitat, the body which governed the Pitiusas from 1299 to 1715. The **Capella del Salvador**, now the reception area, has a splendid 14th-century vaulted ceiling.

The chapel was occupied by the seamen's guild until 1702. Part of the exhibition is located in the **Baluard de Santa Tecla**, from where there are wonderful harbour views. Visitors can also see part of the 14th-century fortifications through a glass panel in the floor. The museum shop sells postcards and reproductions but no glossy publications. A free explanatory leaflet with ground plan is available in English and other languages. *Reial Curia closed for renovation. Archaeological Museum. Open: Apr–Sept, Tue–Sat 10am–2pm & 5–8pm, Sun 10am–2pm; Oct–Mar,*

Gothic ceiling of the Capella del Salvador, now part of the archaeological museum

Tue–Sat 10am–1pm & 4–6pm, Sun 10am–2pm. Admission charge.

Plaça de la Catedral
In the Middle Ages the buildings around this square were occupied by the island's institutions of government. On the corner of Carrer Major is the **Reial Curia**, where the judges and notaries had their offices. The Gothic door beneath

Enjoy lunch on the terrace in Plaça de la Vila

GETTING THE BEST FROM DALT VILA

Before setting out, get hold of a copy of the free large-scale street map from the tourist office. Take your time – Dalt Vila is for savouring. Avoid the afternoon crush and come early in the morning when you'll find it easier to negotiate the engaging labyrinth of lanes, alleyways, ramps and stairways. Return for a romantic stroll after dark when the precincts are illuminated and the atmosphere is hushed and relaxed. Perhaps round off the experience with a meal in El Olivo or one of the other fine restaurants on Plaça de la Vila and Sa Carrossa.

the tower was originally a window. The coat of arms belongs to Felipe V, the Spanish monarch responsible for abolishing Ibiza's autonomy in the 18th century. Next door to the Curia is the Museu Arqueològic d'Eivissa I Formentera.

Plaça de la Vila
While only just inside the fortress walls, Plaça de la Vila is the real heart of the Upper Town where cafés, boutiques, art galleries and exclusive restaurants draw large crowds to the terraces outside the simple, whitewashed frontages. During the day, visitors are entertained by fire eaters and flamenco dancers, but after dark, when the square is illuminated, it has a still, magical quality even though many of the shops remain open. Just off the Plaça de la Vila is the **Baluard de Sant Joan**. From the garden there are views of La Marina and the harbour.

During the 1st century BC the Roman geographer Diodorus Siculus wrote of 'ports worthy of mention, great walls, as well as a considerable number of admirably built houses. Foreigners of all classes live there, mostly Phoenicians.' He was describing the Carthaginian colony of Ibosim (Eivissa), founded, according to tradition, in 654 BC. Carthage was itself a Phoenician colony, dating from the 9th century BC. The Phoenicians were a seafaring people, originally from what is now Lebanon. They were traders rather than empire builders, and they established outposts throughout the Mediterranean. However, by the end of the 6th century BC, the Carthaginians had outgrown Phoenician tutelage and were building their own network of colonies along the coast of North Africa, in Andalucia, Sicily, Sardinia and southern France. In the process they created a distinctive Punic civilisation (the name derives from their dialect). To the Carthaginians, Ibiza was a natural resource to be exploited. The original Phoenician settlement of Sa Caleta was abandoned in favour of Ibosim, a large, natural harbour which became an important strategic point in the western Mediterranean, a nexus of trading routes. They fortified the city walls and built a settlement on the hillside of Dalt Vila down to the shoreline, where evidence of shops and houses has been discovered. A cluster of ceramic workshops suggests that an artisanal quarter existed near what is now Avenida de España. The Carthaginians capitalised on the salt

pans at Ses Salines and they mined silver and lead at S'Argentera (*minium*, a red oxide extract, was used for painting pottery). More lucrative was the export of a purple pigment derived from whelks and used to dye Roman togas. Ibizan pine forests were an important source of wood for Carthage's shipbuilders. Even most of the crops (cereals, figs, olives and fruit) found their way overseas. Able-bodied islanders were hired as mercenaries, acquiring a fearsome reputation as sling-throwers. Ibiza thrived. The island minted its own coins and industrial production increased. Amphorae, used for transporting rough wines and oils, have been found in many parts of the Mediterranean. But the greatest trawl of artefacts has been unearthed on Puig des Molins: vases, coins, necklaces and amulets, terracotta figurines, polychrome ostrich eggs and surgical instruments.

Puig des Molins was a highly-prized place of burial, because of the absence of poisonous snakes and marauding animals – a prerequisite for a necropolis. Wealthy Carthaginians from all over the empire paid handsomely to have their bodies interred here. The site's religious significance can be appreciated from the large number of effigies of the Punic deities. By far the most important of these was Tanit, goddess of love and fertility. Her symbols included doves, palm trees, grapes and the crescent moon. No evidence has been found, however, of the Carthaginian practice of child sacrifice, attested to again by Diodorus Siculus.

Opposite: Ancient tombs in the necropolis, Puig des Molins
Above: Clay statuettes of the Carthaginian deities

Finally at rest – monument to the turbulent crusading knight, Guillem de Montgrí

Plaça d'Espanya

At the centre of this cobbled square, shaded by palm trees, is a monument to Guillem de Montegrí, the aristocratic archbishop of Tarragona who led the conquering Catalan-Aragonese expedition in 1235 and administered part of the island thereafter, albeit *in absentia*. Given Montgrí's martial credentials, it seems almost perverse to present him in a recumbent posture, as here, rather than on horseback.

Portal de Ses Taules

Visitors enter Dalt Vila through the magnificent 16th-century portcullis, a typical Renaissance set piece. Above the 'Gate of the Tablets' is a carving in stone relief of the Hapsburg coat of arms of Felipe II of Spain. The Latin inscription on the tablet underneath praises his achievements and recalls the official completion of the fortifications in 1584. In niches flanking the gateway are two headless marble statues, copied from Roman originals and recovered by a military engineer during the construction of the fortress. One represents the goddess Juno, the other a Roman soldier. The drawbridge spanning the dried-up moat looks the part but is actually a replica of the original and was installed only in 1990. Inside the gateway is the colonnaded **Pati d'Armes**, a courtyard-cum-guardroom where soldiers warmed themselves on chilly winter nights at the open hearth near the entrance. The doorway at the end is decorated with the coat of arms of Catalunya and Aragón. After the rebuilding of Dalt Vila in the 16th century, the Pati d'Armes served as the town market.

Sa Carrossa

The carriages which passed along this important thoroughfare in days gone by gave it its name. At the centre of the street is a bronze bust of the Ibizan historian, poet and priest, Isidor

Macabich (1883–1973). Just about every town on the island has a street commemorating this important local figure, descended from a family of Croatian merchants. Macabich began life as a journalist on the *Diario de Ibiza*. After his ordination in 1907, he was appointed Cathedral archivist, a post he held for many years. He is the author of numerous historical works, culminating in a definitive four-volume *History of Ibiza*, which appeared in the 1960s. Near the statue is a eucalyptus tree which inspired some of his verses. Of the bars, coffee shops and restaurants on Sa Carrossa, 'La Muralla' (right at the top) is popular with gays, who meet here before heading off to the Anfora nightclub (*see pp102–3*).

Vila Nova

The 'New Town' is approached via Dalt Vila's only surviving Arab gateway, **Sa Portela**. (Look for the left turn shortly after Carrer Sant Ciriac becomes Carrer Major.) The new town includes Plaça d'Espanya, Plaça de la Vila and the Baluard de Santa Llúcia, the last of the bastions to be completed.

On Carrer de Santa Maria is the El Corsario hotel where the last of Ibiza's great privateers, Antoni Riquer, lived in the early 19th century.

The Pati d'Armes has a charm of its own

Walk: Exploring Dalt Vila

This walk introduces you to Dalt Vila, Eivissa's stunning walled town, declared a World Heritage Site by UNESCO. Along the way to the Gothic cathedral and the castle at the summit are splendid noblemen's houses and tiny irregular *plaças* lined with restaurants, boutiques and café terraces. The walk requires only a moderate amount of stamina, although there are quite a few steps to negotiate along the way.

The starting point is the main entrance at Portal de Ses Taules, the best point of access from Sa Penya and La Marina.

Allow 3 hours.

1 Porte de ses Taules

Two Roman statues preside over either side of the gate; one represents the magistrate, Caius Julius Gatulicus, the other, Juno, queen of the gods and the Roman equivalent of the Punic goddess Tanit. Above the entrance is the coat of arms of the Hapsburg dynasty to which Felipe II of Spain belonged. Cross the drawbridge (rebuilt in 1990 from old photographs) to the Pati d'Armes, an arched courtyard which served as a kind of guardroom. The smaller gateway at the end leads in to Plaça de la Vila.

2 Town hall

Turn left onto Sa Carrossa, past the statue of Isidor Macabich, a distinguished local historian, to the Baroque church of Sant Pere and the former Dominican convent which is now occupied by the Town Hall. Turn onto Plaça d'Espanya and look out from the ravelin to the lighthouse across the bay on the Botafoc peninsula.

3 Streets of the old town

Make the gentle ascent up Carrer Per Tur, a street lined

Dalt Vila is best explored on foot

with historic mansions. When you reach the former seminary, cross Carrer Joan Roman and climb the steps past the legendary El Corsario hotel, once a pirate's den. Cross Carrer de Santa Maria and take the next flight of steps on the left to Carrer Major. On your right you will see the Gothic doorway of the Reial Curia where Ibizan justice was dispensed in the Middle Ages.

4 Museum of Archaeology
On the left is the Museum of Archaeology. Located in historic buildings adjoining the bastion of Santa Tecla, it has an interesting collection of Punic and Roman artefacts found in various sites on Ibiza and Formentera.

5 Cathedral and castle
Cross Plaça de la Catedral to the Cathedral (open to the public) and the Diocesan Museum (closed for restoration). Behind the Cathedral is the Baluard de Sant Bernat which offers panoramic views of the town, harbour and surrounding countryside. Now turn round and take a look at the castle. Although it was heavily restored in the 18th century, you can still make out a rectangular tower which was part of the original *Almudaina* or Moorish keep.

6 Sant Ciriac
Return via Carrer Major, Dalt Vila's 'high street', which leads into Carrer Sant Ciriac. The small shrine on your left is where the Catalan army broke through the Moorish defences on Sant Ciriac's Day in 1235.

7 Plaça de la Vila
Take the steps down to Carrer Conquista, past the El Palacio hotel. At the end, turn right, passing the white-washed walls of the 15th-century Església de l'Hospital, to Sant Lluis, then left down Escala de Pedra. At the bottom is Plaça de la Vila with its lively café terraces and restaurants.

Extramuros (Beyond the Walls)

Until the beginning of the nineteenth century, Eivissa was confined to Dalt Vila and the two medieval neighbourhoods of La Marina and Sa Penya. This changed with the creation of Vara del Rey, an elegant boulevard only a few minutes' walk from Puig des Molins. This is the one 'must see' in the modern town, sometimes referred to as The Extension (s'Eixample). Most visitors get no further than the bus station on Avingida d'Isidor Macabich, although the new town is a good place to get to know the locals. The prices are lower here, too.

Fisherman at the helm

La Marina

Immediately below the walls of Dalt Vila, in the shadow of the Baluard de Sant Joan, is the old fishermen's quarter, now crammed with restaurants, bars and fashion boutiques, open all hours of the day and night and geared exclusively to the tourist market. To the east of the ramp leading to Ses Taules is the fish market (**Mercat des Peix**), an octagonal building dating from 1875. Also worth a look is the old fruit and vegetable market (**Mercat Vell**) on Plaça de sa Constitució, a handsome structure with a façade of Doric columns. The locals fight shy of paying the high prices here, preferring the unromantic new market on Carrer d'Extremadura. You could stop for a coffee in one of the cafés on the square or move on to the 19th-century **Teatro Peyrera** on Carrer Comte Rosello. No longer a theatre, it is now an important venue for jazz concerts and other musical events. The foyer doubles as a café (*see p155*). **Església de Sant Elm** (Carrer de sa Creu; look for the tiered bell tower) was the church of the guild

View of La Marina from the Baluard de Sant Joan

of seafarers and ships' carpenters. The
original chapel was razed to the ground
by pirates in 1578, just before the new
town defences were completed. On 16
July La Marina's fishermen honour a
centuries-old tradition by sailing into
the harbour with a statue of the Virgin
and Child usually on display in the
church (open only for services). Boat
excursions to nearby beaches depart
from the **Estació Marítima** building on
the waterfront. The obelisk here
commemorates the last of the great
Ibizan corsairs, Antoni Riquer (*see box*).

Sa Penya

La Marina leads without interruption to
Sa Penya, another historic quarter of
red-roofed, whitewashed houses. Gaze
down on it from the Baluard de Santa
Llucia and it will become clear why
this precariously-sited working-class
neighbourhood is called 'the crag'. A
picturesque warren of cobbled passages
and steep alleyways
accessed by stone
staircases, Sa Penya
also makes its living
from tourism. The
bars and garish
boutiques along
Carrer de la Mare
de Déu are
especially popular
with gay visitors,
although everyone
is welcome. Stick to
the well-lit areas at
night, as Sa Penya
has a reputation for
crime and drug
dealing.

ANTONI RIQUER ARABÍ (1773–1846)

Born in Sa Marina, Riquer went to sea at an
early age and quickly established a
reputation for skilful seamanship among his
fellow corsairs. Officially credited with
capturing no fewer than 100 French and
British vessels, his greatest exploit occurred in
1806 when, against overwhelming odds, he
overpowered a 250-tonne British brig, the
Felicity, in full view of patriotic locals gathered
on the quayside. A bit of a romantic, on
hearing in 1831 that the Spanish General
Torrijos had been captured after leading a
coup against the reactionary ruler, Fernando
VII, Riquer attempted to free him from the
prison in Malaga where he was being held.
After Torrijos was executed, Riquer himself was
accused of treason, but pardoned in view of
his valuable services to the Spanish crown.

The exotic surroundings of the Mao rooms, a popular pre-clubbing bar

Head in the direction of the tourist office in Eivissa and you will come across a stone obelisk known as the 'Monument to the Privateers'. It commemorates the Ibizan corsairs who for centuries fought off foreign pirate attacks, defending the islanders as well as the possessions of the Catalan and Spanish crowns. The most famous of these swashbuckling heroes, Antoni Riquer (1773–1846), is honoured in the adjacent square. Corsairs first assumed their role of guardian angels in the 14th century. The war chest of the local authority, the *Universitat*, was simply too small to organise its own military expeditions. Recognising the fact, the Catalan government began issuing registration certificates which gave the holders a powerful incentive: capture an enemy pirate vessel and four-fifths of the plunder is yours. Not surprisingly, there was no shortage of volunteers, and this lucrative form of private enterprise became big business. The corsairs had a fearsome reputation, but so did the enemy. For more than three hundred years, the main threat to the islands came from the Barbary States of the North African coast, where the pirates were given carte blanche to harass the Christian populations of the Mediterranean. Setting out from the safe havens of Tripoli, Tunis and Algiers, they used hit-and-run tactics, arriving in fleets of up to twenty ships, briefly occupying a weakly defended port before sacking the town and beating a hasty retreat. Any inhabitants they didn't murder they took prisoner, for ransom or to be sold into slavery. The secret weapon of the Barbary pirates was the *jabeque*. A pinewood vessel with a sleek hull, powered by three sails, it was light, quick, and, above all, easy to manoeuvre. And when cannon were fitted in the 17th century, it became virtually invincible.

Alarmed by the growth of Turkish power in the Mediterranean (the Turks and

12

EL CORSARIO

the Barbary States were allies), and the devastating impact on commerce, the Christian rulers of western Europe were finally spurred into action. In 1554, the year in which the dreaded pirate-admiral Barbarossa destroyed Maó harbour in Menorca, Carlos I of Spain authorised the rebuilding of Eivissa's defences. His son, Felipe II, was entrusted with overseeing the work, both here and in Santa Eulària which had only recently succumbed to a devastating pirate attack. Subsequently, a system of watchtowers, known as *atalayas* from the Arab word for sentinel, was established to protect the coastline. These huge bastions were manned by *talaiers*, watchmen who, on spotting an enemy vessel out at sea, lit a warning fire (smoke by day), to alert the neighbouring tower which duly passed on the message. Forewarned, the peasants in the surrounding countryside would head for the safety of the newly fortified churches, where the defenders were concentrated.

By the mid-17th century, the corsairs were finally gaining the upper hand,

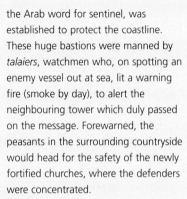

thanks to the development of the *jabeque-polacra*, a much larger, and better armed, version of the Berber prototype. The naval defeat of the Turks at Lepanto in 1571 staved off the Ottoman threat. The improved island defences were also a deterrent, to such an extent that in 1697 the decision was taken to recolonise Formentera, which had been uninhabited for centuries. In 1828 the corsair fleets were officially disbanded. Two years later, the French occupied Algiers and the Barbary pirates lost their main base in North Africa. At last, the people of Ibiza could live in peace.

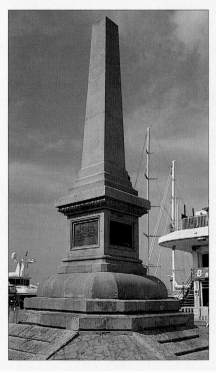

Opposite: Once a pirates' den, the El Corsario is now a hotel
Left: The Monument to the Privateers is a waterfront landmark

Figueretes the palm-lined promenade

Passeig de Vara de Rey

This handsome boulevard, completed in 1912, was designed by the Mallorcan architect, Josep Aloner. The focal point is a monument to the Ibizan General, Joaquin Vara de Rey, killed in action in 1898 during the disastrous war with the United States in which Spain lost the last of her overseas colonies. Vara de Rey's heroic exploits at El Caney, Cuba, when he led his troops against overwhelming odds before falling to an enemy bullet, captured the popular imagination. The statue was paid for by public subscription and there is even a square named after the general in Madrid. Vara de Rey is where the locals buy their newspapers in the morning, returning later in the day for the traditional *paseo* (evening stroll) and a drink on one of the café terraces. For that reason, tables are at a premium – get there before 9pm if you do not want to be disappointed. Alternatively, try the cafés on **Plaça des Parc**, the shady, traffic-free square to the south. There you can admire the neoclassical town houses from the small terrace outside the Sunset Café which serves excellent breakfasts to a faithful clientele of Ibizans and foreign residents.

Platja des Figueretes

This small suburban beach, encroached on by apartment blocks and hotels, is just fifteen minutes' walk from Eivissa town centre. Crowds are guaranteed on the sands during the summer months, but the palm-shaded promenade makes for a pleasant stroll at this or any other time of year. There are views of Dalt Vila to be enjoyed from the car park on Carrer Ramon Muntaner.

Puig des Molins

The best-preserved Punic cemetery discovered to date contains as many as

The Ibizan general, Vara de Rey, leads his troops into battle

4,000 tombs from all points in the Mediterranean. It was chosen specifically because Ibiza was free of poisonous snakes and other creatures harmful to man. The burial chambers were looted as a matter of course until well into the 20th century. Even so, the finds – amulets, necklaces, gold collars, funeral masks, mirrors, painted ostrich eggs, amphorae, and much more besides – are extraordinary and attest to the prosperity of this intriguing civilisation. A nine-storey museum (Museu Monografic) was built alongside the site to house the exhibits, but maddeningly it has been closed for restoration for some time, and so far funding from the Balearic government has not been forthcoming. In the meantime, those interested will have to make do with the representative sample in the Archaeological Museum in Dalt Vila (*see p47*). Visitors are allowed onto the site to see one of the chambers which contains around a dozen stone sarcophagi. The Department of Culture organises free guided tours of Puig des Molins and the mill at Des Porxet (ask at the tourist office for more details).
Puig des Molins, Via Romana 13.

Platja d'en Bossa

During the summer there are regular ferry services from Eivissa to this unashamedly brash, overdeveloped resort where the main attraction is the longest sandy beach on the island 3km (2 miles), with not much in the way of shade but excellent water-sports facilities. Apart from families with children, Platja d'en Bossa's biggest fans are the clubbers, who usually head

straight for the Space dance club (open all day) or the equally famous Bora Bora beach bar. Strung out along the back of the resort is a seemingly endless line of pubs, bierkellers, supermarkets and fast-food outlets. Hardly an oasis of peace and quiet then, even without the roar of aircraft engines making their descent to the airport. Just inland from the beach is the church of **Sant Jordi de Ses Salines**, its crenellated walls a reminder that this was once an integral part of the defensive system which guarded the salt pans (*see p118*). The side chapels were added in the 18th century when the pirates had ceased to be a problem. Sant Jordi is one of the oldest religious foundations on the island, dating from shortly after the Catalan Conquest. The present church was erected in 1577 and restored in the 19th century. If you happen to be here on a Saturday, you could call in at the flea market, which is held in the hippodrome, a former venue for trotting races. The market is open all year round.

Port d'Eivissa

The harbour district begins just north of La Marina, on Avda Santa Eulària, and is best explored on foot. Almost every visitor to the island will become acquainted, sooner or later, with the Formentera ferry terminal, a couple of minutes' walk from the tourist office and only a stone's throw from the **Yacht Club** (Club Nautìco). Beyond the roundabout at the start of Passeig de Joan Carles I is the **Casino** and, just inland, the turning for Pacha, Ibiza's oldest night club. Pacha's rival, El Divino, enjoys a superb setting overlooking the **Marina Botafoc** with its shops, restaurants and boutiques. Behind the main road is the protected land of **Ses Feixes**, first farmed by the Moors in the 10th century (*see p59*). Continue along Passeig de Joan Carles I to the **Botafoc Peninsula**, three small islets now joined together by a roadway.

The remains of a Punic cemetery were discovered on Illa Plana, where plague victims were quarantined during the Middle Ages. Guarding the approaches to the harbour is the 300-year-old Botafoc lighthouse, from where there are outstanding views of Dalt Vila and the old quarters of Eivissa.

'Boat show' – yachts at anchor in Eivissa's Club Nautico

Drive: From Eivissa

This drive sets out from the island's capital, to explore the delightful villages and coves of the east and northeast coasts, before heading inland and returning to Eivissa, via the rolling green hills of the Ibizan interior. The round trip is about 90km (56 miles).

Allow one day to enjoy the places to the full.

1 Santa Eulària

Leave Eivissa on the 733 heading north. After 6km (4 miles), turn right onto the road to Santa Eulària. On your right is Roca Llisa, Ibiza's 18-hole golf course, and a series of turnings to the stunning beach at Cala Llonga. Stop in Santa Eulària to visit the fortified hilltop church to the west of the modern town.

2 Sant Carles

The next stop on the road north (6km (4 miles) from Santa Eulària) is the sleepy village of Sant Carles. In the 1960s this was one of the hippies' favourite haunts – one or two of them still patronise Anita's bar, a good place to stop for coffee and a snack.

3 Two diversions

A side road leads from the centre of Sant Carles to the sheltered cove of Cala Mastella. The calm, clear waters of the pine-clad inlet are a good reason for a swim. Hidden from view by the rocks is one of Ibiza's most sought-after *chiringuitos*, Bigotes, famous for freshly caught fish. An alternative to Cala Mastella is to leave Sant Carles in the direction of Cala Sant Vicent. Turn right after 1km to the small fishing hamlet of Pou d'es Lleo where the rock-strewn sands are usually deserted. Either route is an attractive drive, passing through

Lone yacht off Cala Mastella

terraced olive groves and citrus orchards, marked out by drystone walls.

4 The road to Cala de Sant Vicent

Follow the road north from Sant Carles for 5km (3 miles), then turn right, taking the coast road to Cala de Sant Vicent. There are spectacular cliff-top views as the road emerges from the pine forest.

5 Cala Portinatx

Turn left when you arrive in Cala de Sant Vicent and follow the road as it climbs up through a beautiful valley to Ibiza's smallest village, Sant Vicent de sa Cala. The tortuous ascent continues into the Serra Grossa and the municipal centre of Sant Joan de Labritja. Take a right turn here onto another beautiful stretch of road which winds through the forest down to the sea. As you approach Cala Portinatx, look out for the emerald waters of Cala d'en Serra off to your right. The secluded beach is a short walk away (1.5km (1 mile)) – follow the rough track. You may be tempted to stop for a meal in the *chiringuito* here – the surroundings will certainly be quieter than in the busy resort of Portinatx.

6 Balàfia

Leaving Portinatx, the 733 skirts the cliff tops, offering fantastic views of Xarraca Bay before turning inland through a typical Ibizan valley of terraced fields, planted with olive groves and citrus trees. At the junction with the road from Sant Joan, turn away from the village (right) and continue along the main road to Eivissa. After 5km (3 miles) the defence towers of Balàfia come into view. Originally a Moorish settlement, the defences were to protect the villagers from pirates. Next stop Eivissa.

Platjes de Portinatx Portinatx
Cala d'en Serra
Sant Vicent de sa Cala
Sant Miquel de Balansat
Sant Joan de Labritja Sant Carles de Peralta
Cala de Sant Vicent
Es Pou des Lleó
Tagomago
Sant Llorenç de Balàfia
Santa Gertrudis de Fruitera
C-733
PM-810
Cala Mastella
Santa Eulària des Riu
C-731
Roca Llisa Cala Llonga
Eivissa

N
0   5km
0   2.5 miles

Jesús

Barely 2km (1.25 miles) northeast of Eivissa on the Cala
Llonga road, this suburb takes its name from the church of
Nostra Mare de Jesús. Founded in 1466, it was taken over
by the Franciscans when building was still ongoing some
thirty years later. (The Dominicans built a monastery in
Jesús later in the 16th century, but moved within a few
years to Dalt Vila.)

Ibiza Town from Botafoc
Peninsula

Nostra Mare de Jesús stands almost
alone among Ibizan churches in
preserving an artistic treasure
throughout the traumatic period of the
Civil War. The Gothic altarpiece, in the
Flemish tradition, dates from around
1498 and is the work of the Valencian
artists Rodrigo de Osona the younger
and Pere Cabanes. In the main panel, the
Virgin is portrayed suckling the child
Jesus, while a pair of angels sing their
praises. Note the panel above, where
St Francis of Assisi
exhibits the bloody signs
of the stigmata, a clear
indication that the work
was commissioned by
the Franciscans. There is
little else to detain you in
Jesús, apart from a few
roadside bars and the
Croissanterie Jesús,
which serves breakfast to
exhausted party-goers
on their way home from
the Privilege and
Amnesia nightclubs.
*Església de Nostra Mare
de Jesús. Open: Thur
10am–noon.*

Platja de Talamanca

Just to the north of Eivissa, Talamanca
bay is hidden from view by the Botafoc
lighthouse. The 2km (1.25 miles) long
strip of fine, white sand attracts fewer
visitors than one might expect given its
proximity to the town, and the beach is
freer of development than its rivals to
the south, though there are plenty of
places to eat and drink. The promenade
makes for a pleasant stroll – if you have
binoculars you can home in on the sleek

Dalt Vila, reflected in the waters of the Botafoc marina

A self-indulgent day at Platja de Talamanca

yachts which often anchor here in preference to Eivissa. Watersports enthusiasts will want to check out the windsurfing school. If Talamanca does not appeal, pick up the track at the back of the beach and head for the secluded cove of Cala Roja, just beyond the headland at Cap Martinet. The name 'Rocky Cove' fits the bill perfectly but this is an idyllic spot for a swim with a little bit of shade from the pines clinging precariously to the cliff. If the idea of a 2km (1.25 miles) walk sounds excessive you could take the hourly bus from Eivissa (summer only) – pack a picnic and make a day of it.

Sant Rafel de sa Creu

The hamlet of Sant Rafel occupies a green hillock 7km (4 miles) from Eivissa on the road to Sant Antoni. There are stunning views of Dalt Vila (and most of the southern coast) from the whitewashed 18th-century church. Opposite is Clodenis, one of the island's gourmet temples, renowned for its Provençal cooking (*see p168*). Sant Rafel's other claim to fame is its pottery workshops. You will find them on the village high street – the old Sant Antoni road – no more than a five-minute walk from the church.
Church open only for services.

SES FEIXES

This area of wetland near Talamanca beach was farmed by the Moors more than a thousand years ago. Masters of agricultural technology, they created a highly sophisticated irrigation system of dykes, lock gates and water channels, enabling them to grow cabbages, onions and other crops. Ses Feixes (literally 'The Plots') remained under cultivation until the first wave of package tourists began arriving in the early 1960s. An important bird sanctuary, the entire marsh was declared an 'area of special ecological interest', although this classification has now been challenged by Eivissa town council which wants to allow limited urban development on the land.

Santa Eulària and the East

Ibiza's third largest town, Santa Eulària des Riu is beautifully situated in a serene bay, bounded by gently sloping, pine-forested hills. The fortified hill settlement of Puig d'en Missa, one of the most important urban monuments on the island, is a 'must see'. Santa Eulària is an excellent base for excursions to other parts of the island. Boats leave from the harbour for the hippie market at Es Canar and the beaches of Cala Pada and Cala Llonga. There are regular bus services to Eivissa and Sant Antoni, but only one a day to San Carles and its attractive village church.

A splash of colour at Es Canar beach

Cala Llonga and Sol d'en Serra

Seven kilometres south of Santa Eulària, in a narrow inlet sheltered on two sides by towering pine-clad cliffs, is the insensitively developed mini-resort of Cala Llonga. Its setting is as magnificent as its beach, a 200m (656ft) sweep of fine, white sand. The water, unruffled and almost translucent, is perfect for swimming. There's no shade, though, so bring plenty of sun block and hire a beach umbrella if you don't have one of your own. Water sports available include windsurfing, water-skiing and parasailing – there's also a diving school. Eating and drinking isn't a problem either, in a resort boasting half a dozen restaurants and a couple of *chiringuitos*.

If the crowds begin to pall, it's a pleasant stroll from Cala Llonga to the shingle-and-pebble beach at Sol d'en Serra. Turn right at the La Criolla

restaurant, then follow the road until it becomes a bumpy dirt track. Signs from here will point you in the direction of the bay, less than a kilometre away. The views of Formentera are the main draw

Bargain hunter at work – the hippie market

– enjoy them at your leisure from the terrace of the Sol d'en Serra café-restaurant.

Es Canar

The weekly 5km (3 miles) excursion from Santa Eulària to the Hippie Market at Es Canar is one of the most popular on the island. The absence of genuine hippies – the flower children who sold their wares here in the 1970s have long gone – and the fact that authentic, locally made items are not easily come by, will disappoint the purists. For everyone else there's plenty of fun to be had browsing the more than 400 stalls in search of that elusive present or holiday souvenir. Kaftans, floppy hats, batik sarongs, leather moccasins, trinkets and watches, bongos and tom-toms, you'll find them all here. If you do intend buying, bring cash as few stallholders accept credit cards. The market is near the centre of the resort, in the grounds of the Club Arabí holiday complex. You can get there by bus or car, though driving is not advisable in July and August when the roads are clogged with traffic and parking can be a problem. A more relaxing option is to take the ferry from Santa Eulària. One reason to linger in Es Canar is the Blue Flag beach, a crescent of fine yellow sand, gently shelving and safe for swimming. The small harbour, though, is hemmed in by hotels and apartment blocks, and the bars and restaurants are unenticing.

Hippie Market. Open: May–Oct Wed 10am–7pm; bus from Santa Eulària or ferry (May–Oct).

Pine-covered cliffs shelter the magnificent beach at Cala Llonga

Walk: A Stroll from Santa Eulària

To get the most out of this 6km (4-mile) walk, take your time and fit in a swim or perhaps a cup of coffee along the way. The route follows a well-worn coastal path from Santa Eulària, ending up in the family resort of Es Canar, best known for its hippie market.

Allow 2 hours.

1 Santa Eulària

The walk starts in Santa Eulària, the main resort on Ibiza's east coast. Start by walking along the attractive promenade at the back of the town beach. Stop to admire the sleek yachts berthed in the marina, then continue on the path which leads towards the cliffs.

2 Punta de s'Església Vella

From the 'Old Church Point' there are superb views back towards the marina and the modern town and also across Santa Eulària bay in the direction of Punta de s'Aguait. You won't see any sign of the church, though – it has long since disappeared. The path now skirts the multistorey Los Loros Hotel on the way to the bay known as Ses Roquettes. The roads here were laid out for holiday homes which fortunately were never built.

Pedalos are for hire at Cala Pada

3 Sa Caleta

The urban development along this stretch of the coast (mainly villas) is discreetly hidden by tree cover. Beyond is the prettily named Cala Niu Blau, 'Blue Nest Cove', a 100m (328ft) stretch of fine sand with a café but little else.

4 Cala Pada

This attractive bay is a popular destination for families taking the ferry shuttle from Santa Eulària. There are a couple of beachside cafés here if you have built up an appetite, and you may even be tempted to go for a paddle in the shallow, transparent water.

5 Cala s'Argamassa

From Cala Pada, the path continues past the cluster of modern hotels which constitute the mini-resort of s'Argamassa. At the Florida campsite the path turns inland to cross the rocky promontory of Punta Arabí from where there are fine views of two islets, Rodona and its larger neighbour, Illa de Santa Eulària.

6 Es Canar

The Club Punta Arabí dates from the early 1970s and spawned the famous hippie market which you could visit if you happen to be here on a Wednesday. Otherwise, stroll on to Es Canar, a busy but nevertheless beautiful cove with a Blue Flag beach and excellent watersports facilities. You can now either return to Santa Eulària on foot or hop on a ferry (summer only).

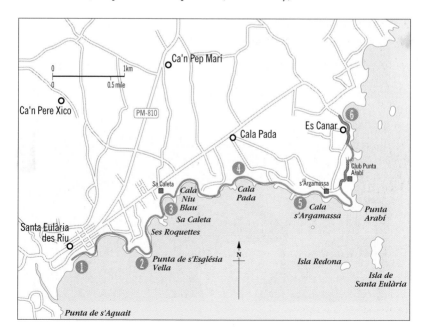

Hippies

Disillusioned with capitalism, the rat race and the consumer society, the 'flower power' generation of the 1960s dreamed of an alternative society based on peace, love and communal living, a spiritual world at one with nature. Some found it in the souks and kasbahs of Marrakech, others in the temples of Goa or the mountains of Nepal, still others found paradise in two small Mediterranean islands.

It all started in 1958 with the opening of Ibiza airport. First came the beatniks, then the hippies, a colourful collection of idealists and dreamers, mystics and gurus, rebels and dropouts, 'Beat' poets and psychedelically inspired artists, peaceniks and draft dodgers fleeing the war in Vietnam. The hippies' hedonistic philosophy was light years away from the dour conservatism of the Franco era, but Ibiza was too remote and unimportant for the dictator to take much notice. Its attractions in those days were even more obvious than now. Of course there was the sunshine, the beaches and the scenery, but back in the 1960s the roads were deserted, the coastline was undeveloped and one could get by on virtually nothing.

(played by Mimsy Farmer) and her doomed love affair with a naïve German student (Bulle Ogier). The British rock band, Pink Floyd, supplied the sound track and the psychedelic tale achieved cult status, especially in France, where it created a minor sensation. Ibiza was now 'hip' and celebrities, like Polish film director Roman Polanski and sixties pin-up Ursula Andress, began buying holiday homes on the island.

The dream was destined not to last. In 1968, 41 hippies were deported after being found guilty of drug dealing and 'immoral conduct'. Few tears were shed by the native islanders who, amused and indulgent at first, had come to tire of their 'dirty' lifestyle and drug-induced antics. By the early 1980s, the tourist boom was pushing prices through the roof, while the commercialism the hippies so despised was now rampant. A few determined souls stayed on, but most left to pursue more conventional careers and lifestyles. But the hippie legacy can still be detected in the Ad Lib fashion movement, the New Age drumming rituals at Benirràs, the hedonistic excesses of the clubbers and the markets at Es Canar and Las Dahlias. Without the hippies, Ibiza and Formentera would have been very different places.

The first hippie haunts were the Can Tiruit commune in Sant Joan de Labritja and the Fonda Pepe bar on Formentera. The folk singer Bob Dylan stayed here for a while before moving on to El Pilar de la Mola. Another popular hangout was Anita's bar in Sant Carles, just down the road from the hippie market at Las Dahlias. Naked revellers held impromptu 'love-ins' on the beach at Es Cavallet or worshipped the setting sun at Benirràs. In 1973, the shrewd owners of Club Punta Arabi agreed to allow half a dozen stallholders to sell their wares on the patio, and the Es Canar market was born.

More

It was a movie by the French director, Babet Schroeder, which put the islands firmly on the hippie trail. *More*, shot on location in Formentera in 1969, was the story of an American drug addict

Left: A mature hippie bangs the drums for Ibiza
Above: Psychedelic view? Kaleidoscopes on sale in the hippie market

From Cala Nova to Es Figueral

You'll have to walk or cycle the short distance from Es Canar to the wild and desolate beach at **Cala Nova**, the perfect spot for a contemplative stroll. There's a campsite nearby, but few families venture down as the rocky shoreline is not well-suited to children. It's possible to swim, although windsurfing is a more popular pastime when conditions are right. Snacks are available from the *chiringuito* at the back of the beach during the summer. If you're here out of season, bring a picnic – the chances are you'll have the place to yourselves.

Cala Nova

Just around the headland from Cala Nova is **Cala Llenya**. Llenya means 'wooded', and older residents remember a time when the area was a mass of pine trees. They're now confined to the back of the beach, a crescent of white sand, hemmed in by low cliffs. When the weather turns blustery the windsurfers arrive (boards are available for rent here). Three kilometres (2 miles) further on is **Cala Mastella**, one of the most delightful spots on this stretch of coast. The bay is formed from two coves which give the small beach of ochre sand an intimate feel. This is a great place for a swim, and if you've built up an appetite the temptation to linger over a seafood lunch at Joan Ferrer's restaurant, El Bigotes may prove irresistible. Once rested, you could take the scenic coastal road from here to Cala Boix, a long narrow strip of dark, pebbly sand. To get down there you'll need to be fit, though – access is via a flight of stone steps carved out of the rock. Beyond the

One of the coves of Cala Mastella

promontory of Cap Roig (Ibiza's most easterly point) is **Cala des Pou des Lleó**, a picturesque spot where the fishing huts are a reminder of older Ibizan traditions. 'The lion' is a reference to the Roman legion once stationed here, while 'pou' is the small spring which is the focus of a religious procession on 8 August. The clear waters and interesting rock formations attract snorkellers. Follow the steep path up from the beach to inspect the *atalaya* (defence tower). It was built to observe the island of Tagomago, once used as a base by Barbary pirates preparing to raid Santa Eulària. From Pou des Lleó you can drive on to **Es Figueral**, a small resort popular with families. The beach is nearly 300m (984ft) long and there are invigorating walks along the coast. From here it's only a short hop to **Aigües**

Blanques, the island's oldest nudist beach.

Beyond Punto Arabí

On the other side of Es Canar, past the wooded headland of Punto Arabí, are more enticing coves and beaches, popular with families and day trippers from Santa Eulària. There are splendid vistas of the rocky islets of Rodona and Santa Eulària from **Ca na Martina**. Scuba diving expeditions set out from here to explore the red coral that thrives around the underwater caves. Equally busy and more developed than Ca na Martina, **Cala s'Argamassa** has a small sheltered beach, liable to be crowded in season. Watersports range from pedaloes and banana boats to parasailing. The mini-resort of **Cala Pada** is only a three-kilometre drive from Santa Eulària but the boat excursion (summer only) is a more relaxing alternative. The main attraction is the 200m (656ft)-long sandy beach where young children enjoy paddling in the shallows. There are several café-restaurants to choose from and excellent watersport facilities, including parasailing, diving and windsurfing. The local sailing school hires out catamarans.

Cala Pada is bustling with watersports enthusiasts

Walks from Cala Llonga

It is possible to reconnoitre the cliffs on either side of the inlet at Cala Llonga. The first route, to a blowhole on the northern side, takes about an hour and a half and is a fairly easy climb along a tarmac road and a well-worn footpath. The second route up to the cliff top at the southern end of the bay is a bit more demanding, but worth the effort for the commanding views of the south of the island.

Allow 3 hours.

PART 1

1 Bay views

Head north along Cala Llonga high street towards the edge of town, taking the side turning up the hill by the supermarket. Turn left at the top and continue up the hill, passing the El Dango apartment complex on your right. From the higher reaches there are superb views across Cala Llonga bay.

2 Blowhole

At the point where the road divides, take the right fork and continue as far as the roundabout. From here take the path heading off into the woods and up onto the cliff. As you emerge from the tree cover, you will see a small cave with a blowhole at the bottom. It's a bit of a scramble down, but worth the effort to watch the sea spray shoot up the vent under pressure from the waves below.

3 Punta Roja
Stroll on towards the end of the peninsula and you will be rewarded with views as far as the island of Formentera and along the coast to Santa Eulària.

PART 2
4 Two views
Leave town on the road behind the Cala Llonga Hotel. Continue along the same route as the road becomes a track, threading its way up the thickly wooded hill and turning completely back on itself several times. The first *mirador* (viewpoint) overlooks Formentera and Santa Eulària Bay. The second is a stunning rearward look at the emerald waters of Cala Llonga. Unfortunately, the track peters out shortly beyond this point.

5 The lookout
Take the footpath directly in front of you, which bears slightly left as it enters the woods. It is narrow and sometimes overgrown in places, but the route is marked at regular intervals by piles of stones. Follow the path to the top of Cap des Llibrell. At 222m (728ft), this vantage point was of great strategic importance. It was known to the Moors, and was regularly manned by sentries on the lookout for pirates. Its last visitors were Nationalist troops during the Civil War. The panorama is a full 360°, but keep away from the cliff edge as it is a sheer drop down to the rocks below.

Safe haven – yachts enter the tranquil bay of Cala Llonga

Santa Eulària des Riu

Santa Eulària's compact new town (Sa Vila Nova) was laid out in the 1940s on a grid pattern, making it easy to find one's way around. Its detractors criticise it for being bland and short on atmosphere. Certainly life here is lived at a more sedate pace than in Sant Antoni or Eivissa (the absence of nightclubs keeps the ravers at bay), but for many visitors this is a distinct advantage.

Road train, Puig d'en Missa

Santa Eulària is a family resort

The focal point of the new town is the Passeig Marítím, a palm-fringed promenade with a decorative fountain, antique gas lamps and immaculately kept miniature gardens. A leisurely stroll will bring you to the Puerto Deportivo, the largest marina in the Pitiusas with more than 750 berths. This is not the place to shop for bargains or dine out on the cheap, but it does boast the only nightclub in town. The local diving school is also based here and boat charter is available at a price. For most visitors, Santa Eulària's greatest asset is not the marina but the gently shelving town beach, a dazzling expanse of whitish sand directly below the promenade. Families, especially those with young children, decamp here in numbers and spaces are at a premium by lunchtime. If you do intend spending time here, bring some head cover and plenty of high-protection sun block as there are no beach umbrellas for hire.

Santa Eulària boasts the only proper river in the Balearics (hence 'des Riu'), but anglers won't find much to write home about as it is bone dry for most of the year. Situated at the river mouth, **Platja Es Riu** is the closest alternative to the town beach. There are a couple of restaurants here and, if you're an early riser, you can watch the sunrise as the fishermen unload their catch (Es Riu is sometimes called the mariner's beach). For a pleasant pre-dinner stroll, follow the landscaped course of the river upstream as far as the old bridge (no more than a few hundred metres).

The most promising streets for restaurants in Santa Eulària are Carrer Sant Jaume (good for tapas) and the parallel Carrer Sant Vincent. Both issue out of Plaça d'Espanya, an attractive square where flowering oleander and hibiscus offer a dash of colour. The monument here pays tribute to the bravery of Santa Eulària's fishermen,

Plaça d'Espanya from Passeig de s'Alamera

who saved the shipwrecked crew of the *Mallorca* from drowning in 1913. The pedestrianised Passeig de S'Alamera is the focus of a mini hippie market every day except Wednesday and Sunday. Basket weaving, ceramics and other Ibizan handicrafts are showcased here and in the adjoining side streets. To describe Santa Eulària as a centre of culture would be gilding the lily, but it was the long-time home of a minor Impressionist painter, Laureano Barreau (*see p77*). The largest commercial gallery, Alfredo, is a couple of minutes' walk from the marina on Carrer de Mar, and in December and January local daubers showcase their work in the Art Supermarket exhibition (details from the tourist office). If you are exploring the town with children in tow, one way to coax them into a bit of sightseeing is to hop on the 'Santa Eulària express', a miniature train which ventures into the Ibizan countryside before ending up at Puig d'en Missa, with a refreshment stop and opportunities to visit the church and museum.

Puig d'en Missa

Santa Eulària's disarmingly beautiful old quarter is ten to fifteen minutes' walk from the new town. It is difficult to believe nowadays, but until the 20th century this *was* Santa Eulària. It was the Romans who first bridged the river and stationed a garrison in the area, though they never built a settlement. Neither did the Arabs, who preferred farming the surrounding countryside, well irrigated in those days by the *riu*.

Only after the Catalan conquest did local farmers begin building houses on the slopes of the hill, around a Christian chapel dedicated to Santa Eulària (first mentioned in 1305). This was razed to the ground by marauding pirates in 1555, stirring Felipe II of Spain into re-fortifying the settlement. The Berbers tested out the new defences in 1621 but were repulsed, and from then on the inhabitants were allowed to live in peace. The Puig d'en Missa visitors see today has barely changed since the 18th century when it comprised (apart from the church) five streets, a fountain and a flour mill. Taken together it is an architectural

Historic Puig d'en Missa towers over the resort

The simple beauty of Puig d'en Missa Church

gem, its stark simplicity to be savoured and contemplated.

Visitors first arrive at the portico or *porche*, which was added to the church in the 17th century. After the hill climb, it makes sense to rest for a few moments beneath the beamed roof, supported by gleaming whitewashed arches and massive pillars. The Italian military engineer, Giovanni Battista Calvi, is usually credited with the design of the church, little more than a nave and apse – the two side chapels, doubling as transepts, were added around the same time as the porch. The thickness of the outer walls means that temperature and humidity levels are constant throughout the year. Sad to relate, nearly all the interior decoration was destroyed in a fire during the Civil War. The present Spanish Baroque high altar comes from a church in Segovia, while the image of

the patroness dates only from 1940. Stop by the cemetery to admire the magnificent views of the town and bay before taking a look at the bastion adjoining the church. This lookout tower has no inner rooms and was accessed via a ladder on the church roof where cannon were placed. Don't leave Puig d'en Missa without visiting the Ethnological Museum on the Can Ros estate, a typical, flat-roofed Ibizan house of the kind which fascinated architects Le Corbusier and Josep Sert. Fully restored, the exhibition space serves as the perfect introduction to a way of life which has now all but disappeared. Visitors enter via the *porxo* or hall (the main living space), before moving on to the kitchen, the wine cellar, the 'trull' where olive oil was produced, and the sleeping quarters. The rooms contain fascinating displays of jewellery,

A breathtaking view over Sant Carles de Peralta

costumes and espadrilles, toys and musical instruments, fishermen's gear, agricultural and carpentry tools – there's even an original corsair's licence. You can see craft demonstrations (wickerwork, embroidery, and so on) during the summer months.

Museu Etnològic d'Eivissa i Formentera. Open: May–Oct Mon–Sat 10am–1pm & 5–8pm; Nov–Apr Mon–Sat 10am–1pm & 4–6pm. Admission charge.
Església de Puig d'en Missa (church). Open: daily May–Sept 9am–9pm. Free.

Sant Carles de Peralta

As there are only two bus services a day during the week to Sant Carles and only one on Saturday, it makes sense to drive the 7km (4 miles) from Santa Eulària, perhaps stopping along the way to buy some of the produce from the local farms and market gardens. Sant Carles itself is little more than a cluster of whitewashed houses and a church dating from the beginning of the 19th century. The building is locked more often than not, so you are unlikely to get much further than the porch, a double arcade of doughty columns supporting a pine-timbered roof. While you are cooling off here or maybe writing a postcard, spare a thought for the local curate, executed by the Republicans in the early months of the Civil War when the church was ransacked and its furnishings destroyed.

Signs near the bus stop point the way

to **Anita's Bar**, still trading profitably on its 1960s hippie associations. The Ibizan liqueur, *herbes eivissenques*, and a range of appetising meals are served up on the covered terrace, a more attractive option than the rather gloomy dining room. Anita's also doubles as the local post office.

Take the Santa Eulària road from Sant Carles and on your right (ten minutes on foot) is **Las Dahlias**. The hippie market here, while smaller than Es Canar, has a more authentic feel – there is more than a whiff of cannabis about the place. Browse the stalls for handmade kaftans, beaded handbags, cashmere shawls, silk pyjamas, statuettes of Indian goddesses, African drums and the like. Plump up a cushion in the souk-like café and you could be heading down the road to Marrakech. Alternatively, call in at the pub restaurant and ask the locals about the hippies who made good – some bought *fincas* in the area, spot the Porsche. Las Dahlias is open all year,

and during the December Christmas Market visitors are treated to hot snacks and glasses of mulled wine.

S'Argentera

The countryside around Sant Carles is remarkably unspoiled and so peaceful that you can drive for miles and not hear anything but birdsong. If you are tempted to linger, head for the *mirador* at S'Argentera, 110m (361ft) high, from where there are panoramic views across the coastline. S'Argentera means silver, a curious misnomer as it was lead that was mined on the hillside here from Roman times. Puig de S'Argentera is now a miniature nature park. Leave the car in the car park, pick up a map and follow any of the trails through the pine woods. You may stumble across some of the mine workings which were not finally abandoned until the early years of the 20th century.

Es Trui de Can Andreu

Follow the road from San Carles to Cala Llenya and within a couple of minutes you will come to this well-preserved *casament* or farmhouse, now converted into a small but appealing museum. The name Es Trui refers to the enormous olive press on show in the kitchen, without a doubt the prize exhibit. The owner takes visitors on a guided tour of the house and there is a shop selling local wines.

Hand plough on display outside Es Trui de Can Andreu

Walk: Exploring Santa Eulària des Riu

A circular walk, starting on the promenade in Santa Eulària and taking in the old settlement of Puig d'en Missa. We have allowed time for a leisurely coffee break en route. The modern municipal capital dates only from the beginning of the 20th century and was laid out on a grid pattern in the 1940s. The focal point is the Town Hall on the leafy Plaça d'Espanya.

Allow 2 hours.

1 Riu de Santa Eulària

The only river in the Balearic region is hardly worthy of the name. In medieval times the Riu flowed freely, irrigating what was then highly fertile land. Now, though 11km (7 miles) long, it is little more than a trickle for much of the year. Happily, the local council had the bright idea of landscaping the banks near the estuary with gardens, a small park and a children's play area.

2 Paseo Marítimo

Stroll along the palm-lined promenade past two arcs of fine, white sand – the Platja des Riu (river beach) and the smaller (but busier) town beach. The sheltered waters of Santa Eulària bay are

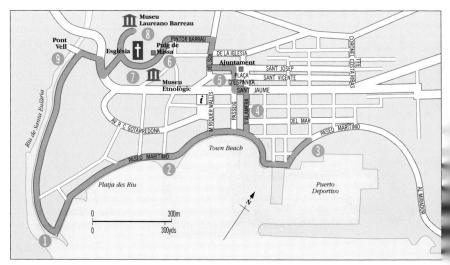

ideally suited to jet- and water-skiing – aficionados of both sports practise on the river beach.

3 Puerto Deportivo
The marina at the northern end of the promenade is the largest in the Pitiusas. The restaurants and shops are pricier than those inland, and unless you are feeling particularly flush you probably won't want to linger.

4 Passeig de s'Alamera
Return to the promenade and turn right onto the wide, leafy avenue known as Passeig de s'Alamera. This pedestrianised street is the heart of Santa Eulària's shopping area, and is good for souvenir hunting.

5 Plaça d'Espanya
At the top of Passeig de s'Alamera is Plaça d'Espanya, a small square dominated by the colonnaded façade of

Souvenir shopping at Passeig de s'Alamera

the Town Hall. On the corner of Sant Jaume is The Royalty, a café-restaurant dating back to the 1930s. They serve late breakfasts on the terrace as well as cakes and ice creams, so this is an ideal place to put your feet up for a few moments.

6 Puig d'en Missa
Turn left onto Carrer Sant Josep (behind the Town Hall), then right onto Carrer Sol. When you reach the produce market bear left onto Carrer Pintor Barrau and start the steepish climb past picturesque whitewashed houses to Puig d'en Missa.

7 Two museums
There are two small museums on the hill. The more immediately appealing is the Ethnology Museum on the Can Ros estate. Next to the church is the house of Laureano Barreau, a Catalan Impressionist who liked to paint the Ibizan countryside, especially the coastline around Santa Eulària.

8 The church
At the top of the hill is the 16th-century fortress church complete with circular defence tower. From here there are panoramic views of the town and bay.

9 Pont Vell
Take the footpath which starts 50m (164ft) above the Ethnology Museum and leads down to Carrer Sant Jaume. Turn right here, then, after another 50m (164ft) or so, bear left onto the path which leads to Pont Vell, a 17th-century bridge with three stone arches, now used only by pedestrians. Follow the footpath beside the river to return to Riu Beach.

Serra de Els Amunts

The pine-carpeted massif of Els Amunts covers an area of around 100sq km (39sq miles) from Cap Nunó to Sant Vicent. The relatively heavy rainfall here makes it one of Ibiza's most fertile regions – wine, olives, almonds and lemons all thrive on the terraced hillsides. Approaching the coast, the scenery becomes more rugged and dramatic, the crags and stacks of the sheer cliffs inhabited only by cormorants, peregrine falcons and Audouin's gulls.

Cala d'en Serra

Since 1991, most of the coastline has been protected as an area of special natural interest and is perfect for hiking. The area also boasts some of Ibiza's most beautiful coves, many of which are sufficiently off the beaten track to deter the package tourists based in the built-up resorts of Sant Miquel, Portinatx and Sant Vicent.

Cala Benniràs

There are stunning views from the coastal road skirting this pearl among coves. Take care with the descent as the path is especially slippery after rain. One of Benirràs' attractions is the absence of hotel development. Another is the fine expanse of pebbly sand at the end of a long inlet, sheltered by pine-wooded hills. The rocks on either side of the bay make it a paradise for snorkellers. The amenities are more than adequate: showers, umbrellas, sun loungers, a *chiringuito* and a couple of restaurants. It was the mystical associations of Benirràs that attracted the hippies back in the 1960s. Fellow travellers still make the pilgrimage on the August full moon when they drum through the night for world peace.

Cala Xarraca enjoys an idyllic setting

Cala des Portixol

One of Ibiza's more isolated coves, Cala des Portixol is well worth tracking down. It can be reached by car with a walk to follow. (There is no *chiringuito*, so pack a picnic.) From Sant Miquel de Balansat, take the road west in the direction of San Mateo, turning off at signs to Isla Blanca. Just beyond the holiday homes is Manolo's bar (closed out of season). Leave the car here and follow the dirt track. After about 30 minutes you will be rewarded with wonderful coastal views towards **Cap Rubio** ('Blond Point', 315m (1033ft)). Sea birds perch in niches in the fissured cliffs, and if you have binoculars you may catch a glimpse of the rare Eleanora's falcon. Tucked away in the small inlet down below is a pebbly beach with a cluster of fishermen's huts but little else. Arrive before lunch and the chances are you will have the place to yourselves.

Cala Xarraca

Between the holiday resort of Portinatx and Sant Joan de Labritja lies Xarraca, an expansive bay with three excellent beaches. The rocky shores and transparent waters are an open invitation to snorkellers; bathers, however, should tread carefully on the sea bed. **Cala Xarraca**, the busiest of the three, also has the most room – the mud baths to the west do wonders for the skin tone. Next door is **S'Illot des Renclí**, named after a tiny offshore islet. You may see fishermen dragging their boats onto the shore here – some of the catch will be served up to patrons of the cliff-top restaurant. An inviting prospect, the more so given that **Cala Xuclà** – without question, one of the most beautiful spots on the island – is a mere stroll away. The superb setting and remote location are an instant recommendation to anyone seeking peace and solitude, but come early in the season – Xuclà's charms are no longer a secret.

Nature works its magic in the San Marca cave (*see p80*)

Strolling through the streets of Sant Miquel is a treat

Cova de Can Marça

This 100,000-year-old cave system was formed by a river burrowing under the hillside. It is of interest to naturalists as well as geologists, since bone and fossil remains of long-extinct species have been found in the rock. In more recent times, smugglers used the caves to hide contraband liquor – they found an entrance below the present one and hauled themselves up with the aid of ropes and hoists. There are spectacular views as one makes the steep descent from the café terrace (and ticket office) to the entrance, approximately 12m (40ft) above the sea. (Vertigo sufferers may want to give this one a miss.) The guided tour – in English – lasts about 20 minutes and is rounded off by a set-piece sound and light show around an artificially created cascade suggesting the appearance of the chamber and galleries in the dim and distant past.

Port de Sant Miquel

The lovely pine-wooded approach to this busy resort, about 5km (3 miles) from Sant Miquel de Balansat, offers few hints about what lies in store. For more than 30 years, the view to one side of the bay has been marred by an ochre-coloured hotel with extensive terraces. Port de Sant Miquel caters more or less exclusively for German and British holiday makers, especially families with young children. This is reflected in the menus of the resort's plentiful bars and restaurants. Sant Miquel's most obvious asset is its gently shelving, sandy beach where there are excellent opportunities for watersports. There is no shade, though, and precious little elbow room by the end of June. If the crowds cast a pall, try your luck elsewhere. **Caló des Moltons**, to the west, has a *chiringuito* and beach umbrellas and is accessible on foot. Alternatively, you can drive to **Es Pas de S'illa des Bosc**, which takes its name from a small offshore islet. Set back from the cliff is an 18th-century *atalaya* (watchtower), Torre de Mular.

Portinatx

Ibiza's most northerly resort has shed the last vestiges of Spanishness in the quest to lure ever more foreign visitors. During the season, day trippers on 'round the island tours' disgorge onto the largest of the three beaches, **S'Arenal Gros**, from the coach park opposite. The shops and restaurants trailing up the hill offer the predictable tourist fare of burgers and pizzas so if this prospect fails to entice, continue in the direction of **Cala d'en Serra**. Within ten minutes you will be enjoying the fragrance of the pines, still abundant in this part of the island. The 7km (4 mile) hike to the beach should take no more than an hour and a half – drivers will have to walk the last 200m (656ft). Snacks are available from the *chiringuito* and there are umbrellas and sun loungers for hire. Bring a pair of sandals and watch out for the rocks when swimming.

Portinatx is one of Ibiza's most popular resorts

A walk in the woods exploring the country park at Can Pere Mosson

Sant Joan de Labritja

Two banks, a post office, a mini-market and a petrol pump – on the face of it, not much to detain the visitor, in this village on the road from Eivissa to Portinatx. Yet there is more to Sant Joan than meets the eye, for example the paradox that a community of around 400 people should have its own town hall. In fact, Sant Joan is a municipality covering more than a third of the island. The parish church was completed around 1770, except for the belfry (c.1900) which purists have criticised for being out of keeping with the whole. Sant Joan was a focus for the hippie community in the late 1960s. One German visitor who discovered the island in those days went on to found the Eco Centre, an Internet café with an attractive garden terrace, just across the road. Eco also runs an organic market and a New Age bazaar and organises everything from car hire to entertainment at children's parties.

Sant Llorenç de Balàfia

Stop long enough in the village to admire the stark geometrical minimalism of the church, then head off to the real point of local interest, about 1km (0.6 mile) to the east on the Eivissa to Portinatx road. Balàfia derives from an Arab word meaning 'health-giving fountains', a clue to the mediaeval origins of the place. As late as the 16th century, this was the *only* inland settlement of any importance on the island, a distinction which did not escape the notice of the North African corsairs. When they were sighted off the coast (usually in the dead of night), a patrol would set off cross-country to inform the inhabitants of this mini-citadel. The thick, interconnected walls of the half-dozen houses (still inhabited today) are a reminder that they were as much a part of the defences as the sturdy ochre-coloured bastions – the lime crosses were to ward off evil spirits. As in Santa Eulària, would-be assailants were bamboozled by the absence of a door – access was via an upper-storey terrace on which a ladder was planted when the need arose. Take the Es Figueral road from Balàfia and you will pass Ca na Pepeta, a restored *granja* (farmhouse) serving excellent, reasonably priced regional cooking. The Can Pere Mosson nature park occupies the wooded hill above the church at Sant Llorenç. There are marked hiking trails and barbecue areas with pleasing views of the surrounding countryside.

Sant Mateu d'Aubarca and around
The wild, remote stretch of coast from Cala d'Aubarca to Cap Nunó has, mercifully, escaped the attention of the developers, largely because of the stony

> ## PUNTA DE SA CREU
>
> This spectacular *mirador* offers one of the finest views on the north coast. To get there, follow the road north to San Miquel, then take the signposted turning to the Hotel Hacienda at Na Xamena (the only five-star hotel on the island). To the right, a rough surfaced road branches off in the direction of the coast. To the west of the headland is Portixol and Cap Rubió; to the east, beyond Port de Sant Miquel and the Can Marça caves, lies the magnificent cove at Benirràs. Not even the heliport can intrude on the beauty of the spot.

beaches. Cala d'Aubarca is best reached on foot (from Sant Mateu, take the Cami d'Aubarca road at the church – if you are driving you will have to walk the last kilometre or so). In the Middle Ages falcons were bred here, and they still nest in the clefts of the rock. To the left, behind the headland at **Cap d'Aubarca**, are two ruined bastions and a section of broken wall, all that remains of the **Torres d'en Lluc**. The origin of these defences, which probably date from early mediaeval times, is shrouded in mystery. It has been suggested that they were intended to ward off

Medieval tower stands guard over Balàfia

Sant Mateu is an up-and-coming wine growing region

attack from enemies on another part of the island rather than to guard the coast. The cliffs at Cap Negret are the tallest in Ibiza at 375m (1,230ft). To get to the *mirador* here, follow the Can Gorra path from Santa Agnès. To the east, beyond Cala d'en Sardinia, is **Punta de ses Torretes**, a tooth-like promontory with a cleft just wide enough for small boats to pass through. Offshore are a couple of tiny islets known as Ses Margalides, breeding ground of the Ibizan green lizard. A side turning 2km (1.25 miles) off the Santa Agnès–Sant Antoni road leads to the **Cova des a Vi (Ses Fontenelles)**. The cave paintings discovered here in 1917 were originally thought to date from the Bronze Age (2nd millennium BC). An alternative theory is that the depictions of boats (unfortunately badly weathered) are Punic, the authors possibly being watchmen guarding the lookout tower at Cap Nunó. The cave is closed to the public for the foreseeable future.

Sant Miquel de Balansat

By common consent, the parish church of this small village, built on a hill 175m (574ft) above sea level, is among the most beautiful on the island. Founded shortly after the Catalan invasion in the 13th century, it is also the oldest, although nothing of the original building survives. A gateway with a triple arcade leads to a spacious inner courtyard, like the thick walls, designed to ward off enemy attack. The overall harmony of the building is the more surprising given that the nave was not completed until the end of the 17th century. The wall frescos date from the same period. Every Thursday evening during summer, the Colla de Balansat dance troupe performs outside the church.

Santa Agnès de Corona and around

Between San Mateo and the pretty hamlet of Santa Agnès lies the fertile Corona Plain, planted with olives, citrus trees, vines and almonds which flower in

January and February scattering white and pink petals over the encircling hillsides. The young, but eminently palatable, wines produced here have long been valued by the locals and are now gaining recognition further afield (*see p170*). There are no official tours but the owners of the Bodega Sa Cova, about 1.5km (1 mile) west of Sant Mateo, are happy to show visitors around with advance warning. The village also hosts a wine festival in December. Five kilometres (3 miles) from Sant Mateo, Santa Agnès is a pleasant spot to stop for refreshment, though there is little to see apart from the diminutive church (1806). On the square, *bocadillos* filled with cheese and mouthwatering *serrano* ham are the speciality of Bar Costa, where the walls are decorated with paintings from the flower power era – the artists were broke so they paid in kind.

Sa Cova Estate, tel: (971) 187 046.

Santa Gertrudis de la Fruitera

As its name suggests, fruit growing has long been the mainstay of this small agricultural community. In recent years well-heeled townies have been building second homes in the vicinity, which accounts for the boutiques and art galleries. If you are interested in antiques and bric-a-brac, check out the website of the English auction house, Casi Todo ('almost everything') for information about the monthly sale. Terrace bars and restaurants cluster around the main square, by the typical fortified church (1796).

Casi Todo:
www.casitodo.com

Santa Agnès de Corona from Cafeteria c'an Cosmi

The 303m (994ft) peak of Sa Talaiassa towers over Sant Vicent de Sa Cala

Sant Vicent de Sa Cala and around

There are two scenic routes to Cala de Sant Vicent, one following the pine-wooded road from Sant Joan, the other negotiating a tortuous corniche with breathtaking views of the bay and the island of Tagomago. Down below, sheltered by the hills, is the beach, a

DEATH ON THE BEACH

In 1936 the body of Raoul Villain was found on the beach at Cala St Vicent with a bullet through the throat. A right-wing nationalist, Villain was the assassin of the great French socialist, Jean Jaurès. After being acquitted in 1919, thanks to the chauvinistic climate in France at the end of World War I, he bought a house in Ibiza and went into hiding. But the Spanish Republicans caught up with him during the Civil War. His whereabouts were betrayed and, after a summary interrogation, he was killed.

perfect arc of fine sand, 400m (1312ft) long and 40m (131ft) wide. The setting is undeniably magnificent, though the hotels and holiday villas that have accumulated here over the years tend to detract from the natural beauty of the bay. Cala Sant Vicent has excellent water-sports facilities (snorkelling, diving and water-skiing, for example), but essentially this is a family resort. During summer, boats leave on excursions to Tagomago and the beaches at Es Figueral and Es Pou de Lleó. The nudist beach at **Aigües Blanques** (popular with gay visitors) is also nearby. To get to the stony but virginal cove of **Port de ses Caletes**, at the foot of Puig de Sa Fita 308m (1,010ft), you will have to take the signposted road from Sant Vicent de Sa Cala – little better than a rough track in places – then walk. There is no beach to speak of or anywhere to eat or drink, but the mirror-clear waters, sheltered by towering cliffs, are ideal for swimming and scuba diving. By far the best way to explore this area is on foot. Pick up a map from the tourist office and follow the blue signs along the Ruta des Falcó hiking trail to the hamlet of **Sant Vicent de Sa Cala** (3km (2 miles) inland) where there is little to detain you, apart from a typical Ibizan church, dedicated in this case to the mediaeval firebrand preacher, St Vincent Ferrer (patronal day, 5 April). There is another Ruta des Falcó from the village to **Punta Grossa**, the lofty promontory which shelters Sant Vicent beach. The views along the way are nothing short of spectacular. Just north of Cala St Vicent

is the ancient Carthaginian sanctuary at **Cova des Cuieram**. (To get there, take the paved road from the east end of the bay to the car park, then follow the signs to the cave, a steep uphill climb.) The finds here have been dated to between the 5th and 2nd centuries BC. Copies of the terracotta statuettes dedicated to the fertility goddess Tanit are now on sale in almost every Ibizan gift shop, but to see the originals you will have to pay a visit to the Archaeological Museum in Eivissa. The caves are closed at present, but the views of the coastline are well worth the trouble.

Disarming simplicity – the dazzling façade of Sant Vicent's minimalist church

Walks from Santa Agnès

There are two scenic cliff-top walks from the attractive village of Santa Agnès de Corona. The first heads towards the rugged cliffs of the north coast, before doubling back to Sant Mateu. *Allow 4 hours to cover the 15km (9 miles).* A less demanding alternative is to follow the circular route around the picturesque Corona plateau (about 8km (5 miles) – *allow 2 hours*). Take some water with you, as there are no shops or cafés en route.

PATH TO THE NORTH COAST
1 Valle de Corona

Leaving Santa Agnès by the small lane at the side of the church, you will soon begin to cross the magnificent Corona valley, one of the most fertile parts of the island thanks to the rich reddish soil and sheltered aspect. All kinds of crops grow here, from vines and cereals to lemons, figs and almonds.

The vineyards at Sant Mateu

2 Cala d'en Sardina

When you see a fork in the road after about 1.5km (1 mile), turn left towards the coast. Continue through the wood which becomes denser as you make your way up the hill at the side of the valley. After another kilometre (approx. 0.5 mile) take the footpath branching off to the left which leads to the cliffs above Cala d'en Sardina. Straight ahead is the rocky promontory of Punta de ses Torretes with coastal views to either side.

3 Torres de Lluc

Follow the line of the cliffs towards Cap des Mossons, and at the beginning of the headland you will see the remains of the mysterious Torres de Lluc. No one knows why or when these towers were erected, although it has been suggested that they were part of a fort protecting a coastal settlement (which no longer exists) from possible attack from inland. Stretching below is the majestic bay of Cala d'Aubarca.

4 Sant Mateu d'Aubarca

Take the path from Cap des Mossons

and descend through thick woodland to the Valle de Corona, before taking the left fork to Sant Mateu. Call in at the village bar to sample a glass of the local *vi pagès* wine, before returning along the dirt track through the valley back to Santa Agnès.

THE CORONA PLATEAU
5 Ses Balandres gorge

From the centre of Santa Agnès take the Cami des Pla de Coruna. Where the road bends to the left, turn right onto the farm track. Continue through the wood and the rough track becomes a footpath. After about 1km (approx. 0.5 mile) you'll reach the Ses Balandres gorge. It's a tough, slippery descent to the sea below; better to walk to the *mirador* to the west of the gorge. From the cliffs here you can look out to the crescent-shaped island of Ses Margalides.

6 Pla de Coruna

Take the footpath back through the trees and return to the Cami des Pla de Coruna. Turn right. When the road turns off to the left, continue along the path, keeping to the edge of the fields. The Pla de Coruna plateau, ringed by gently undulating hills, is 200m (656ft) above sea level. The rich palate of colours in the patchwork of fields makes for a good photograph. Follow the path inland as it joins the dirt track again, and at the next junction turn left, back across the fields to Santa Agnès.

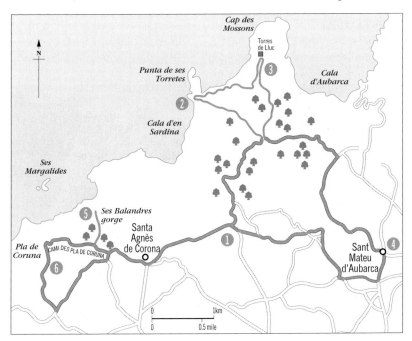

Over millennia the Pitiusas were visited by successive waves of invaders and colonisers – Bronze Age farmers, Phoenician and Carthaginian traders, Roman and Byzantine artisans and craftsmen. A number of sites have already been uncovered, although archaeological knowledge of the islands' history and pre-history remains sketchy. The pick of the finds is exhibited in the Archaeological Museum in Eivissa, and while there is not always that much to see *in situ*, the settings are usually worth a visit in themselves. The tourist office organises guided tours to Puig des Molins (*see p52*), Ses Païses, Sa Caleta, Cova des Cuiram and Ca na Costa.

Ca na Costa

When the megalithic monument at Ca na Costa was discovered on Formentera in 1974, it aroused great excitement among archaeologists in establishing beyond doubt that the Pitiusas had been settled long before the Phoenicians arrived in the 7th century BC – more than a thousand years earlier, in fact. The funeral chamber, a circle of jagged stones, was approached via a rectangular atrium and narrow corridor (originally covered over). Apart from the expected axe heads and bone tools, the remains of eight individuals, six men and two women, were unearthed at the site.

Cap de Barbària

See p124.

Cova des Cuieram

Several pieces of evidence attest to the religious significance of this small cave. Firstly, a Punic inscription was discovered

including houses (originally of more than one storey), store rooms and iron smelting workshops for making tools and weapons. After barely half a century, the Phoenician settlers decided to move the capital to Eivissa and Sa Caleta was abandoned for good. When they left, they took everything of value with them, even cleaning up before they went. *Between Es Condolar and Cala Jondal. The site is open to the public but is surrounded by a metal fence.*

Ses Fontanelles
See p99.

Ses Països de Cala d'Hort
For well over a millennium (450 BC to AD 700) the hillside overlooking Es Vedrà was inhabited by Punic, Roman and Byzantine communities who earned a living from farming and fishing. Finds from the largest of the buildings here, dating from the 1st century AD, suggest that it was put to agricultural or commercial use with storerooms, wine cellars and kitchens built around a large central courtyard. Nearby are the remains of two necropolises, one from the Carthaginian era, the other Byzantine.
About 2km (1.5 miles) from Cala d'Hort, off the Cala Vedella road.

in the 1920s: 'For Abdesmun son of the priest Azarba'al, for our lady Tanit, the powerful.' Secondly, there was evidence of a small altar with a scattering of animal bones suggesting sacrifice. Finally, hundreds of terracotta statuettes of the Carthaginian fertility goddess were found in the recesses of the chamber.
1km (approx. 0.5 mile) north of Cala de Sant Vicent – follow the signed footpath. Open only with official guide.

Sa Caleta
Excavations at Sa Caleta, the first Phoenician settlement in the Pitiusas, were completed in the early 1990s and covered an area of some 4 hectares (9.8 acres/40,000sq m). The colonists, several hundred all told, are thought to have arrived from southern Spain in around 650 BC. Visitors can see the foundations of a number of buildings,

Opposite: The ancient stone circle at Ca na Costa
Above: Finds from historic sites are exhibited in Eivissa's Archaeological Museum

Sant Antoni de Portmany and the West

Ibiza's largest town after Eivissa boasts a magnificent harbour and a nightlife second-to-none. But if clubbing is not the reason you came to the island, use the port as a base for exploring the further reaches of the west coast. Take a stroll in the direction of the marina and catch a boat to one of the three blue flag beaches in the area or head north to the equally alluring coves of Cala Gracioneta and Cala Salada. A boat excursion to the rocky islet of Es Vedrà is the ideal curtain raiser for the Cala d'Hort Natural Park.

Punta des Moli, Sant Antoni

Some history

The cave paintings at Ses Fontanelles point to a human presence in the area during the Bronze Age. The Romans valued the harbour, calling it Portus Magnus ('large' or 'great' port), but it was not until after the Catalan invasion that Portmany was settled by colonists from the mainland under the command of the Count of Roussillon. They farmed the area behind the port, growing wheat, barley and other crops. The fields were irrigated by the Torrent de Buscastell, a stream which flowed into the harbour. In 1305 the Archbishop of Tarragona authorised the building of a chapel dedicated to Saint Anthony, patron saint of animals and agriculture. This was replaced by a fortified church after Portmany was sacked and destroyed by Berber pirates in 1383. The defences were refined over the centuries – there were cannon on the roof until 1869. The modern history of Sant Antoni begins in the 1960s with the arrival of the first wave of tourists in what was then the proverbial sleepy fishing village. The developers went to work with a vengeance, and by the 1980s Sant Antoni had grown into a mega-resort with an unenviable reputation for heavy

'UC'

Visitors to Sant Antoni may notice a statue by local sculptor António Hormigo on Carrer Ramon y Cajal. Completed in 1977, its official title is Es Verro (The Brave One), but everyone refers to it as 'The Shouting Man' because of the hands cupped in front of the mouth. Actually, the subject of the sculpture is making the 'uc', a strange guttural sound unique to the Pitiusas and thought to originate in pre-Roman times. Some suppose it to have been a war cry, others, a primitive form of communication. Ucadors are proud of their abilities and can produce subtle variations in rhythm, pitch and tone.

drinking, drug taking and loutish behaviour, most of the blame laid at the door (with good reason) of the British contingent. The authorities were forced to step in, since when things have quietened down, though the West End still has a somewhat sleazy reputation. 'San An' belongs to the clubbing fraternity in July and August, but families are beginning to return at other times of the year.

The promenade

The palm-fringed promenade (Passeig de Ses Fonts, Passeig de la Mar) was one

The Egg sculpture, Sant Antoni

of the improvements introduced during the 1990s to offset the town's down-market image. Beyond the Yacht Club, which offers sailing lessons, and the 204-berth marina is the Moll Vell, the old dock where fishermen still land their catches. Passeig de Ses Fonts comes into its own on Sant Antoni's two red-letter days, 17 January and 24 August, when the celebrations include a huge firework display. However, you can catch something of the festive flavour on Sundays from November to April when the local folk troupe performs the *ball pagès,* a traditional dance unique to the Pitiusas. Call at the tourist office by the 'egg' (*see panel*) for information about local walks: there are four *Rutas de Falcó* exploring the environs of Sant Antoni and a more demanding 23km (14 miles) hike to Santa Agnès de la Corona, reaching deeper into the surrounding countryside.

MONUMENT TO THE DISCOVERERS

Known irreverently as 'The Egg' the symbolism of this odd-looking monument derives from an apocryphal anecdote concerning the explorer, Christopher Columbus. Looking for a sponsor to back one of his expeditions, and being told that it was impossible, the great man picked up an egg and asked whether anyone could stand it upright. After much shoulder-shrugging on the part of his audience, Columbus achieved just that by cracking and removing part of the base. 'Nothing is impossible' was his comment, and the rest, as they say, is history.

Walk: Platjes des Comte

Only half an hour's bus ride away from the mayhem that is Sant Antoni in the summer is the coastline of the Platjes des Comte, an area of natural beauty under the protection of the Balearic government. This walk takes in some of the best bays and coves and is far from strenuous. There will be plenty of opportunities to buy drinks along the route so you won't need to carry water; however some kind of headgear is essential as there is little shade from the sun.

Allow 2 hours to cover the 6km (4 miles), a little more if you're planning to stop for a swim or a spot of lunch.

1 Platjes des Comte

Buses leave from Sant Antoni for the Platjes des Comte, the starting point of the walk. The beaches of Cala Conta and

Cala Comte

Cala Comte are among the most beautiful on the island, though sand is at a premium along this rocky shoreline. The sea is crystal clear, however, and the coastal views are splendid.

2 Three islands

Start walking from the beaches in a northerly direction across the sandstone cliffs and look out at three islands which form part of the Cala d'Hort Natural Park. The nearest, and smallest, is S'Illa des Bosc. The name means 'wooded isle', although this hardly fits the bill today. To the south lies the long, straggling island of S'Espartar, while to the north, rising like a humpback whale from the sea, is Sa Conillera.

3 Torre d'en Roviras

Follow the edge of the cliff, keeping an eye out for the indigenous green lizard which makes its home in the dry scrubland. Continue to the Torre d'en Roviras, an 18th-century watchtower. From here there are even better views of Sa Conillera and, in the opposite direction, the Bay of Sant Antoni.

4 Cala Roja

Walk on beyond the tower in the direction of Sant Antoni and you'll pass Cala Roja. There is no beach here and the fishermen, whose huts are scattered along the shoreline, are usually undisturbed by visitors.

5 Cala Bassa

Cross the headland at Cap de la Bassa and descend to the cove of the same name (Cala Bassa). The locals reckon this is the finest beach on the island, and the European Union agrees, awarding it Blue Flag status – you may be tempted to stop here for a swim. If you decide to stay longer, there are several café-restaurants to choose from, and in summer boats depart from here for Sant Antoni.

6 Es Penyal

Beyond Cala Bassa the path ascends again to the cliffs at Es Penyal where you might see the storm petrel or the Balearic shearwater; both nest on the offshore islands between March and June.

7 Port des Torrent

Next stop is the busy resort of Port des Torrent, nowadays little more than an extended suburb of Sant Antoni. Torrent refers to a stream that flows down here from Sa Talaiassa, Ibiza's highest peak, before emptying out into the bay. The beach is popular with day trippers and you may find the crowds off-putting, although the terrace of the Can Pujol restaurant makes a pleasant lunch stop. Conceivably you could walk back to Sant Antoni from here, but there isn't much in the way of scenery. It makes more sense to take the bus from the holiday village or the ferry shuttle (summer only).

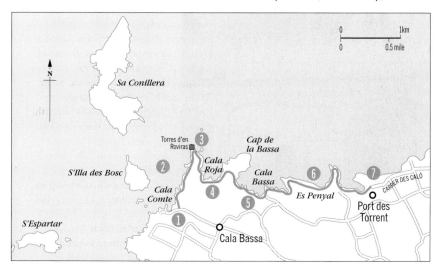

Beaches

For a quick dip, the town beach at S'Arenal or the string of rocky coves further around the bay will suffice. However, the water quality here is not all that it might be – better to explore the more inviting beaches, less than half an hour's journey away by boat or bus. Scuba diving and other water sports are available at various points along the promenade. For other sporting options, *see p160*.

Beach life at Cala Conta

Sa Cova de Santa Agnès

Hidden inside the mouth of a small cave, 1.5km (1 mile) north of town on the Santa Agnès road, is an ancient shrine, thought to date from around the 4th century AD. Interestingly, pottery fragments and other remains have been found from the Punic era, suggesting that this Christian place of worship, one of the oldest on the island, may originally have been a pagan sanctuary. About 100m (328ft) away is an 18th-century church, now the Sa Capella restaurant, which serves traditional Ibizan cuisine.

Cave. Open: Mon–Sat 9am–noon.

Església de Sant Antoni

Although its origins are much older, the present parish church dates mainly from the 17th century, when the splendid polygonal tower was added as a defensive measure. There are two other noteworthy features, the portico to the side of the church and the *azulejos* (painted tiles) which decorate the base of the interior walls. Only the statue of St Antoni survives from a 17th-century retable made for the high altar and destroyed in a fire during the Civil War.

Punta d'es Moli

The rocky promontory at the far end of S'Arenal beach

The 17th-century Església de Sant Antoni

(overlooking Platja des Pouet) takes its name from a flour mill, which has been restored and is open to visitors. You can see the hydraulic machinery for pumping water, the *trull* where olive oil was produced, and a typical villager's house, now occasionally used for exhibitions.

West End

English is the *lingua franca* of this part of town where every other building is a pub selling the great British breakfast, cut-price beer and live sport on TV. After dark the street sellers appear, hawking the predictable range of watches, junk jewellery and sunglasses to would-be customers on their way to one of the noisy discos, the other speciality of the West End.

Sunset Strip

This is the popular name for the parade of up-market bars and nightclubs on the way to the beach at Caló des Moro. The 'old timer' here, Café del Mar, was founded in 1980 and is still going strong. Since 1994 the house DJs have been producing their own 'chillout' CDs at the rate of one a year. Sipping a cocktail on the terrace of Mamba, Savannah or Coastline as the sun sets is a relaxing way to pass the early evening.

Taking in the glorious sunset along the strip

One of Ibiza's best kept secrets, the sheltered cove of Cala Gracioneta

Cala Gració

Sadly, the ravages of the developers have taken their toll on Cala Gració's beautiful setting, while the shimmering expanse of fine, white sand attracts too many visitors at the height of the season when the pleasure boats drop anchor here on their way from the Cap Blanc aquarium. Better to take the path by the fishing huts on the north side of the bay to the neighbouring inlet of **Cala Gracioneta**. The beach here is no more than 30m (98ft) wide, but this is a beautifully sheltered spot, perfect for swimming and with a *chiringuito* serving meals almost at the water's edge. Surprisingly, Gracioneta's existence passes almost unnoticed.

To drive to Cala Gració from Sant Antoni takes a matter of minutes and is hardly worth the effort. A healthier alternative is to cycle or walk, taking the detour suggested by the *Ruta des Falcó*, to the palaeochristian chapel at Sa Cova de Santa Agnès. (Leave Sant Antoni on the Santa Agnès road: *see p104*.) A little further on from Cala Gració is the *mirador* **Cap Negret**, from where there are stunning views of Conillera Island. Nudist sunbathing is possible on the rocky promontory of Punta de sa Galera, between Cap Negret and Cala Salada (follow the footpath from Sa Cova de Santa Agnès).

Cala Salada

This magnificent cove at the end of a pine-forested road is only 5km (3 miles) from Sant Antoni. The beach is off to the right – take the path by the stone tower. Sun worshippers may be happy to bask on the rocks near the boat houses, though it is difficult to see how anyone can resist a dip in the clear turquoise waters. Cala Salada's surroundings are surprisingly unspoilt, given its proximity to Sant Antoni, but, for the same reason, it is unlikely to be deserted. The locals, who need no reminding of its charms, moor their boats here at weekends. It may be difficult to land a table at the fish restaurant, built on a series of terraces near the cliff. Do try, though – the fish stew speciality, *caldereta de langosta*, is mouthwatering. If you are still feeling adventurous, you could take the footpath leading directly from the cove to Puig Nunó, passing the cave at Cova de Ses Fontanelles on the way. It is tough going in places but worth the effort for the wonderful coastal views.

Cova de Ses Fontanelles

The 'cave of springs' is also known as the Cova des Vi because wine was once stored here. The paintings on the walls of the chamber are thought to depict boats although they have been weathered by erosion and are now only faintly discernible. They were discovered by the French archaeologist Henri Breuil in 1917, who dated them to the Bronze Age. More recently, scholars have suggested that they are Punic, pointing out that the Carthaginians built a watchtower on nearby Cap Nunó.
Half a kilometre (0.3 mile) inland from Cala Salada (follow the signs). The cave was badly damaged during building work in the 1960s and is still off limits to the public.

Tranquil Cala Salada, less than 15 minutes' drive from the bustle of Sant Antoni

Beaches to the west of Sant Antoni

Four kilometres (2.5 miles) from Sant Antoni, at the western edge of the bay, Port d'es Torrent is an extension of the town and heavily developed on all sides, except to the rear of the beach where the pines have been left undisturbed. There are umbrellas and sun loungers for hire, and a choice of places to eat and drink, but not much else to recommend the resort. Give this one a miss and head for the twin beaches of Platjes des Comte. Both **Cala Conta** (the larger of the two) and **Cala Comte** enjoy the coveted Blue Flag status, with small stretches of golden sand – no shade, though – and superb snorkelling and diving conditions. Urban development has been kept at bay and there are fine coastal walks through pine-scented scenery (*see p94*). There are bus and ferry services to Cala Conta during the summer, but despite the ease of access relatively few day trippers get beyond

Port d'es Torrent. Closer to Port d'es Torrent and equally well served by local transport is **Cala Bassa**, just around the headland of Punta de Sa Pedrera. The gently shelving beach and sandy sea bed (also Blue Flag) are the big draw for families with young children – pedaloes and banana-boat rides are also available.

Sa Conillera Archipelago

From Cala Comte one can clearly make out three islands of which the largest is. **Conillera** – 'rabbit island' – is the largest. Sadly, the story that this was the birthplace of the Carthaginian general, Hannibal, has been all but discounted. Equally fanciful, but more entertaining, is the folk lore that witches collect the grasses needed for their secret potions here on St John's Eve (23 June). Barbary pirates used Conillera as a base to attack Sant Antoni, which explains the presence of the watchtower on Punta de sa Torre. The 19th-century lighthouse

Splashing around at Cala Conta

Diving for beginners – Sant Antoni is Ibiza's watersports mecca

has a range of 30km (19 miles) and warns sailors of the treacherous reefs lurking in the strait between Conillera and its nearest neighbour, **Illa des Bosc**. Once densely wooded (hence the name), this was the proverbial port in a storm for stranded fishermen, though it looks pretty inhospitable at a casual glance. It was once inhabited by charcoal burners, which explains why the forest is now denuded. The former residents of **Esparter**, the third island in the group, augmented their diet with seagulls' eggs and *virot* chicks (a kind of shearwater). The Conillera archipelago is part of the

Cala d'Hort Natural Park (*see p14*) and an important conservation area. The crevices in the limestone rocks are a breeding ground of the endangered Balearic shearwater (*puffinus mauretanicus*), which was here long before man came on the scene – fossil remains have been discovered from the Pleistocene period. Serious ornithologists organise boat trips to the more remote archipelago of **Ses Bledes**, around 3km (2 miles) further out to sea. A graveyard of merchant shipping from Punic times onwards, Ses Bledes was used by whalers in times gone by.

Clubbing

Ask anyone under 40 to name one thing they associate with Ibiza, and the chances are it will be clubbing. Every year from June to late September the island's dance meccas rock to the 'Ibiza Sound', a catch-all phrase for a bewildering variety of musical styles, spawned by the synthesiser but with little else in common apart from a pounding drum underlay. For many years, dance music was largely a British phenomenon, but Spanish, Italian and German interest is growing, thanks to the commercial success of a handful of party anthems. Dedicated *aficionados* save up for months to be able to enjoy the full clubbing experience. They come for the music, the company, the spectacle, the drugs in some cases, but above all they are here to have a good time – 'largeing it', to borrow from the vernacular.

The Ibiza scene has its origins in the hippie counter-culture of the 1960s, which offered an alternative lifestyle to the repressive Franco dictatorship. The first club, Amnesia, was little more than an overgrown disco operating from a converted farmhouse on the road to San Rafel. The action soon moved out of doors and, as more clubs began to appear, the 'rave' was born. At the same time, the influence of the home-grown 'Balearic Beat' – a mixture of electronic, Latin and Afro funk sounds – on British Acid House in the mid-1980s gave birth to dance music and the clubbing phenomenon. When the island authorities banned open-air partying at the beginning of the 1990s, the clubs responded by taking the action indoors where it became more raunchy and outrageous with each successive season. Rock stars, supermodels and other A-list celebrities began dropping in, and the resultant publicity generated by the

gossip columnists was a godsend for the promoters. Nowadays, you are more likely to see soap stars and game show hosts, but, while numbers have been down of late, there is little evidence to suggest that the clubbing bubble is about to burst. The greatest threat may stem from the cavalier attitude of some club owners to noise pollution and other regulations,

the side of main roads. If you want to know more, you can consult the clubbing monthlies *DJ Magazine* and *Dub*, or browse the club websites (*see p157*). When deciding what to wear, the rule is: the more outlandish the garb, the better. In the world of clubbing anything goes, from basques to cami-knickers, from top hats to platform soles. Think 'fancy dress', and you can't go far wrong. Clubbers get into the swing in the 'warm-up' bars in Sa Penya or Sa Marina (Eivissa) or the 'Sunset Strip' in Sant Antoni. Some promoters, Manumission for example, have their own bars which play ambient or chillout music (laid-back sounds with a funky beat).

which has angered the environmental lobby and many ordinary residents.

A night out

No one is in the dark for long about where the action is. Fliers are distributed on beaches and in bars, while the major events are advertised on hoardings at

Opposite: The Eden nightclub is a paradise for today's Adam and Eve
Above: Fire juggler at Eden

GAY IBIZA

Ibiza, Eivissa especially, is now firmly established as a leading holiday destination for gay men, and there are plenty of gay-friendly hotels and pensions to choose from. For nightlife in Dalt Vila, head for the La Muralla bar, the Anfora nightclub or one of the many gay haunts on Sa Carrossa. The leather bars and boutiques on Carrer Mare de Déu (Sa Penya) are popular gay hangouts, as well as the outrageous Dôme bar near the fish market on Carrer Alfons XII where transvestites and drag queens like to strut their stuff on the terrace. Gays congregate on the nudist beaches of Es Cavallet, especially around the Chiringay beach bar – open summer only – and at Aigües Blanques on the east coast. Most of the mainstream dance clubs advertise gay nights – look out for the promotional literature. For more information, visit *gay-ibiza.net*

Drive: From Sant Antoni de Portmany

The first of two possible routes explores the unspoilt villages of the island's hilly northern interior with stunning views of the countryside along the way. The round trip is about 50km (31 miles). *Allow 4 hours without stops.* The alternative route takes in some of the best beaches of the Cala d'Hort Natural Park. Distance: 30km. *Allow 3 hours.*

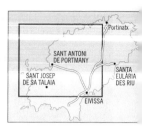

PART ONE

1 Santa Gertrudis

Leave Sant Antoni on the C731 to Sant Rafel – not much to see here apart from the ceramic workshops along the way – then take the scenic Santa Eulària road passing the Hipódromo (racecourse). Turn left at the next junction (5km (3 miles)) and head for the currently chic village of Santa Gertrudis de Fruitera, possibly stopping for a

Try the cove of Cala Tarida for the perfect swim

delicious *jamon serrano* (cured ham) *bocadillo* on the terrace of Bar Costa.

2 Sant Miquel de Balansat

From Santa Gertrudis it is only a short drive to the village of Sant Miquel. Leave the car for a quick look at one of Ibiza's typical fortress churches, perched high above the village on Puig d'en Missa. From the square outside there is a panoramic view of the thickly wooded hills of Els Amunts.

3 Port de Sant Miquel

A scenic 5km (3 miles) diversion from Sant Miquel will bring you to the cliffs overlooking the sheltered bay of Port de Sant Miquel and the Can Marça cove beyond. After visiting the cave, you could head back for a swim in the resort.

4 Santa Agnès

The delightful side road from Sant Miquel to Santa Agnès passes San Mateu, one of the smallest villages on the island, before winding through the Valle de Corona, a fertile plain, where the surrounding hillsides are planted with oranges, almonds and vines – wine growing is a speciality of the area. Santa Agnès is also famous for its tortillas – the Can Cosmi restaurant is a good place to sample them.

5 Cala Salada

Heading south from Santa Agnès, take the road to the right, a scenic, humpbacked route which threads its way back to Sant Antoni. Along the descent you will enjoy spectacular sea views of Cala Salada.

PART TWO
6 San Agustí des Vedrà

From Sant Antoni drive south in the direction of Sant Josep, looking out after 5km (3 miles) for the signs to San Agustí des Vedrà. Time seems to have passed by this tiny hilltop village, which is well worth a detour.

7 Sant Josep

This small, well-heeled town is the centre of the municipality. Its shops, boutiques and restaurants are laid out around a modern square with plenty of shade. There are cash points here too, if funds are running low.

8 Cala Vedella and Cala Tarida

Take the same road out of town, but as you leave the houses behind, take the left fork heading towards the coast. This road offers good views of the pine-covered hillside of Sa Talaissa, Ibiza's highest point. At the next junction turn left again and follow the coastal road to the beautiful coves of Cala Vedella and Cala Tarida, both good for swimming. From Cala Tarida it is a 10km (6 mile) drive back to Sant Antoni.

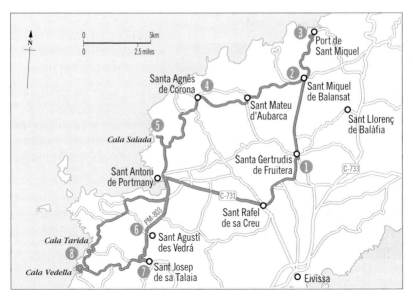

Sant Josep and the South

Sant Josep de Sa Talaia takes its name from Ibiza's highest peak, Sa Talaiassa, from where there are commanding views of the island. The other main attraction of the region is its magnificent coastline, great swathes of which are safeguarded against future urban development. The Cala d'Hort Natural Park extends from just north of Cala Carbó to the rugged cliffs of Es Cubells. The Ses Salines Natural Park centres on the salt marshes which gave birth to Ibiza's oldest industry.

The Torre d'es Savinar lookout

Sant Josep

To take the pulse of this thoroughly modern village – give or take an 18th-century parish church and a 1,000-year-old olive tree – find a table on the shady terrace of Can Bernat Vinye, the pick of the bars on the main square. The locals drop in after Sunday mass for a few hands of *manilla* (a popular Spanish card game), oblivious, it would seem, to the creeping gentrification of their village. Next door is a shop specialising in embroidery, and you will also find a furniture shop where the owner likes to show visitors his interesting collection of folk instruments. Sant Josep's parish church was built by the villagers themselves as a labour of love. Work began in 1726 but was interrupted by an outbreak of plague. Four years later the Valencian architect Pere Ferro was brought in to finish the job – the gallery running above the side chapels is a typical Valencian touch. Of the original Baroque retable, only the wooden figure of St Joseph was saved when the church was gutted during the Civil War. The current altarpiece, a replica, was installed in the 1950s. The *colla de Sant Josep*, one of the best dance troupes on the island, performs regularly outside the church during the summer.

Sant Josep's 3-storey church is one of the most imposing in Ibiza

Es Cubells

The cliffs above Cala d'Es Cubells seem an unlikely location for a church, but in 1855 the local fishermen, tired of tramping all the way to Sant Josep for mass, persuaded their firebrand preacher to build them a chapel closer to home. Father Palau, a Carmelite monk better known for his lonely sojourn on Es Vedrà, consecrated the oratory of Mare de Déu de Carme in 1864. From the road there are awe-inspiring views of the coastline from Cap Negret to Cap Llentrisca and of Formentera beyond. Dotted about the beach are the *chamizos* (thatched huts) where the local fishermen keep their boats. In days gone by this was a doubly dangerous occupation because of the constant threat of pirate attack. This was serious enough in the Middle Ages to deter the people of Sant Antoni from taking up fishing at all.

CELEBRITY HOMES

The Swiss film star Ursula Andress, star of the James Bond movie *Dr No*, was the first celebrity to buy a house in Ibiza – she lives in Es Cubells. Hard on her heels came the film director Roman Polanski, and there are now more than a dozen famous names with property here, including the three-times Formula One motor-racing champion Niki Lauda, 'mother of punk' Nina Hagen, the models Linda Evangelista and Jade Jagger, the rock star Noel Gallagher and Johnny Lee Miller of *Trainspotting* fame.

The pebble beach at Cala d'Es Cubells

Off the beaten track – the charming village of Sant Agustí

Sant Agustí des Vedrà

Bar Berri, Can Berri, and even the formidable-looking parish church, belong to the Berri family. At least it was one of their ancestors who paid for it – on condition, it is said, that the building was re-aligned so that he could see it from his house. Completed in 1806, the buttresses and side tower are clues to its defensive role; likewise the site, the highest point in the village with commanding views across the west of the island. Everything in this one-horse town clusters around the Plaça Major, including Can Berri Vell, the oldest *finca* in Ibiza, now a restaurant serving mouthwatering pâté.

BOAT TRIP TO ES VEDRÀ

Of the boat trips from Sant Antoni, the pick of the bunch is the cruise to Es Vedrà, one of the island's truly awe-

inspiring sights – bring a camera and binoculars. The excursion by glass-bottomed catamaran departs at 3pm every afternoon (summer only) and takes 3 hours. Tickets are available from kiosks on the waterfront an hour before sailing. Demand is high so do not wait until the last minute. The cruise includes a swimming stop. The itinerary for the trip is as follows:

1 Cala Tarida

The boat rounds the promontory at Punta de s'Embarcador, passing three or four inconspicuous inlets en route to the larger bay of Cala Tarida. The broken line of white buildings – small hotels and self-catering apartments for the most part – is all there is in the way of urban development. The rocky end of the beach is good for snorkelling, and scuba diving is also a possibility. The

C'as Mila restaurant serves freshly caught fish from a terrace overlooking the bay.

2 Cala Molí

This small but enchanting cove, almost closed off by sheer cliffs and sheltered by pines and conifers which trail down to the beach of pebbly sand, is relatively quiet most of the time. The hilly countryside of the Serra de Cala Molí is good hiking territory.

3 Cala Vedella

This low-key resort caters mainly for families with young children – the calm waters and gently sloping beach of soft white sand are its obvious assets. Luxury yachts and motor launches anchor off the coast in the late afternoon – the sunsets are special here. There is a walk from Cala Vedella to Ibiza's highest peak, Sa Talaiassa 476m (1562ft) – ask at

Cala Tarida is one of Ibiza's most appealing resorts

the tourist office for the relevant *Ruta de Falcó* map.

4 Cala Carbó and Cala d'Hort

(*See below*)

5 Es Vedrà

The boat makes a complete circuit of this limestone colossus, its near vertiginous cliffs towering 382m (1,253ft) above the sea and the smaller islet of Es Vedranell. Myth and magic are Es Vedrà's stock in trade. They say that this is all that remains of the lost continent of Atlantis and that Homer's hero Odysseus avoided shipwreck after being lured here by the Sirens. For centuries, Es Vedrà was uninhabited except for goats and rabbits. Then, in the mid-19th century, a Carmelite monk, Francesc Palau, came to live here as a hermit and reported seeing 'unearthly beings surrounded by light' – UFOs in modern parlance. More recently, Es Vedrà appeared as the fictional island of Bali Hai in the film version of *South Pacific* and on the cover of Mike Oldfield's album *Voyager*. As the boat rounds the island, train your binoculars on the cliffs for possible sightings of Audouin's gulls, shearwaters, shags, storm petrels and, if you are lucky, Eleanora's falcon. Few boats land here, none at all during the breeding season from 1 March to 30 September.

Cala Carbó

'Carbo' means 'coal' and harks back to the days when the impoverished inhabitants of Conillera brought charcoal for sale in the small port. Since then, the pine woods behind the bay

Es Vedrà from the 18th-century defence tower, Torre de Savinar

have been decimated to make way for building development, but the serene setting still seduces. You will need to get here early, though, as the pebble-and-sand beach is only 50m (164ft) long and fills up quickly. Stay long enough at any rate for a spot of lunch at the Restaurant Balneario. If the *guisat de peix* (a succulent stew made from a selection of fish and cooked with potatoes) is one of the specials, so much the better.

Cala d'Hort Natural Park

Inaugurated in 2002, this protected area extends over 3,000 hectares (12sq miles), embracing the islands of the Conillera and Ses Bledes archipelagos (*see p101*), Es Vedrà (*see p109*), the coastline from Cala Carbó to Es Cubells (*see p107*) and the wooded slopes of Sa Talaiassa (*see p112*). According to local ecologist José Ribas, up to 900 plant species will be conserved, not to mention the fauna and marine life. The natural beauty of Cala d'Hort makes it a location of choice for films and fashion shoots – its fans include celebrities like Goldie Hawn, Jade Jagger, Elle MacPherson and Mariah Carey. However conservation activists are at loggerheads with Sant Josep council over the future of the luxury properties around Es Cubells, including the villa owned by *Oasis* rock band member Noel Gallagher.

The views of Es Vedrà from the shoreline of **Cala d'Hort beach** are best enjoyed over a sundowner on one of the bar terraces. This lovely cove is a major

Dining at Cala d'Hort

draw at the height of the summer, but at other times of the year there is a good chance you will have the place to yourself. The offshore waters have near-perfect visibility to a depth of up to 8m, ideal conditions for snorkelling and scuba diving. There are opportunities to see the *posidonia oceanica* sea grasses, ammonites, cephalopods and other marine fossils, and fish such as wrasses, groupers, sea bream, mullets, rays and octopuses. The schools in Port d'es Torrent and Sant Antoni also organise wreck-diving expeditions in the vicinity of Illa des Bosc.

Torre d'es Savinar

For some unforgettable views, follow the turnoff about 1km (0.6 mile) from Cala d'Hort, then take the signed turning to the *mirador* at Cap des Jueus and the watchtower of Torre d'es Savinar, also known as the 'pirate's tower' since 1909, when it featured in a novel by Valencian writer Vicente Blasco Ibáñez. They say that on a clear day you can make out the Spanish coastline from here. At the base of the cliff is Sa Pedrera, a quarry excavated in the 16th century to build the fortifications of Dalt Vila (*see p32*). More recently, the hippies adopted the place for its karma, renaming it 'Atlantis'. Some are said to have experienced visions of the Buddha here, which inspired one artist to paint his image in a cave.

Rock spiral at 'Atlantis'

Sa Talaiassa

It was the Moors who gave Ibiza's highest peak its name (meaning 'watchtower'), and the panoramic views from the pine-carpeted summit explain why. You should have no problem making out the Bay of Sant Antoni, the salt pans of Ses Salines, the beaches of Es Condolar and Cala Jondal and the islet of Es Vedrà. On the clearest of days you may even be able to spot Mallorca and the outline of the Spanish coast. Sa Talaiassa

The pristine sands at Ses Salines with typical conifer backdrop

is popular with ornithologists who have recorded sightings of hoopoes, golden oriole and woodchat shrikes on the lower slopes, and crossbills and firecrests higher up. The rare Marmora's warbler has also been known to make an appearance. It is possible to drive to the summit, but if you are reasonably fit it is more rewarding to take on the 12km (7.5-mile) hike from Sant Josep (*see p106*).

Ses Salines beaches
There are two fabulous beaches on the fringes of the salt pans, catering for anyone who enjoys music, beach bars, water sports and beautiful surroundings but not necessarily peace and quiet. The nudist beach at **Es Cavallet** has been unofficially adopted by the gay community, while around the headland of Punta de sa Torre is Platja Migjorn, an equally dazzling stretch of white sand, bordered by dunes and pine trees, universally known as Ses Salines. The actor Michael Douglas is one of a number of celebrities who drop in at **Ses Salines'** Trinxa restaurant from time to time. At the western end of the beach, near the bus stop, is **La Canal**, the small jetty where cargo vessels load up with salt, while a path to the rear leads to **Torre de Ses Portes**, a watchtower once armed with three cannon and finally abandoned in the 19th century. From here there are wonderful views of the

islets off the coast of Formentera, including Illa des Penjats (Isle of the Hanged), where executions once took place. Mounds of salt, waiting for collection from the pans, are clearly visible at **Es Condolar**, a beach littered with small stones, hence the name (from *còdol*, a dialect word for boulder). The best views of the pans can be had by walking the 5km (3 miles) from Ses Salines, across the back of Es Falcó 144m (472ft) to Es Condolar. The beach's setting would be idyllic, were it not for the proximity of the airport. At the far end is the tiny cove of **Sa Caleta**. You could combine a swim here (*chiringuitos*, but no shade) with a spot of culture by visiting the ruined Phoenician settlement of the same name (*see p91*). Continue along the coast to **Cala Jondal**, whose sweeping stretch of pure white sand attracts families and young people. Clubbers gravitate towards Tropicana (salsa music), while the beautiful people prefer Bar Particular (rated among cognoscenti as one of the best beach bars on the island). The shoreline is stony, so if you intend to swim, flip-flops are a good idea.

Ses Salines Natural Park

The 400 hectares (988 acres) of wetland between Es Condolar and Ses Portes includes not just the salt pans (*see p118*) but a natural environment with a unique cultural landscape: dunes and beaches, forests of juniper and sabine pines, defence towers, salt warehouses, windmills, water wheels, wells and churches. The Natural Park is an ecosystem under special international protection and centred on the salt pans, a resource which has been exploited for more than 2,600 years. The roads, trails and pathways crossing the area are well signposted, and, as much of the terrain is flat, this is perfect cycling territory. The proposed visitors' centre and car park will be next door to the old salt workers' chapel at Sant Francesc d'Estany, dating from the 18th century. The adjoining cemetery had to be abandoned when it was discovered that the mineral-enriched soil was actually preserving the corpses rather than decomposing them. Take the footpath from the chapel to the Torre de Sal Rossa, one of two bastions constructed by the engineer Giovanni Battista Calvi in the 16th century to guard the salt works from pirate attack. Sal Rossa, literally 'red salt', refers to the pinkish tinge the granular crust acquires after evaporation. Its other name 'de cargador' is a reminder of the longshoremen who loaded the salt here before the building of a new jetty at La Canal.

What you see

The Ses Salines wetlands are an important habitat for nesting water birds and migrators sojourning here on their way to and from Africa. The Kentish plover, the black-winged stilt, herons, storks, flamingos, terns, bitterns, grebes, ospreys, fisher eagles and egrets are among the 205 species that have been recorded in the course of a year. The salt pans are also rich in marshland and ocean-bed plants, molluscs, crustaceans and endemic insect species.

Practicalities

The money for the visitors' centre should have come from the ecotax; however, since this has now been abolished, the fate of the project is uncertain. For the time being, tourist information has maps with suggested walking and cycling routes graded according to difficulty. The most demanding of them covers the 19km (12 miles) from Platja d'en Bossa to Sa Caleta, taking in the beaches at Es Condolar, Es Cavallet and Ses Salines.

Although the terrain is flat, only the fit should attempt the entire route in one day. When walking along the road, keep to the left so you can be seen by oncoming traffic. Bring some kind of head covering and sun block in summer, wear strong, waterproof shoes and never leave without mosquito repellant. If you think you might be out after sunset, take a flashlight for walking in the dark. Cameras and binoculars are another must.

Salt pile, Ses Salines

Walk:
Sa Talaiassa and Around

Nestling prettily in the valley below Sa Talaiassa, Ibiza's highest peak, Sant Josep makes a good base for hill walking. You can call it a day here if you wish, but if you still have reserves of energy and a couple of hours to spare, head for the beautiful coastline around Cala d'Hort. The going is not particularly tough, but you will need to set out early to avoid the full heat of the sun. Wear sensible footwear and bring a hat, sun block and water, as there are no shops or cafés en route.

Allow 2 hours for the 6km (4-mile) hike from the village to the summit.

A stunning sunset over Cala d'Hort

1 Farmland

Leave Sant Josep on the Sant Antoni road. After about 2km (1.25 miles), turn left onto the signposted Sa Talaiassa track, a pleasant trek through walled citrus orchards and olive groves. On the way you will pass the Capella de S'Accident, a small chapel which commemorates the victims of an air crash which occurred here in 1972. Cheats drive to the top, so keep an eye out for cars en route.

2 Sa Talaiassa

As you approach the summit, the scenery becomes more rugged. Only the sturdy sabines seem to thrive in the rocky soil. The area around the radio mast has too much tree cover for views, but there are plenty of gaps a little lower down. On an exceptionally clear day, you might be able to make out Mallorca to the north and the Valencian coast of mainland Spain to the west. At the very least, you can see Ibiza spread out below you and Formentera beyond.

3 Ses Roques

You can either return to Sant Josep at this point or retrace your steps back down the hill as far as the fork to Ses Roques. This forested path leads to another vantage point, overlooking Cala d'Hort and the Es Vedrà rock. If you are here between April and November, look out for fleeting appearances of the Eleanora's falcon, a rare bird indigenous to the Balearics.

4 Cala d'Hort

From Ses Roques retrace your steps in the direction of Sa Talaiassa, looking out on the right for the signposted path which will lead you on a steady descent down towards Cala d'Hort. To get to the beach itself you will have to turn left onto the Cala Vadella road, then turn right. By the time you reach this legendary beach, famous for its transparent water, its sunsets and its views out to Es Vedrà, you will have earned a swim. Now you will have built up an appetite; fortunately, there are several *chiringuitos* to choose from. The pick of the bunch is Es Boldado, but you may have to book ahead to get a table here.

Salt Pans

When the Ses Salines Natural Park was created in 1995 it marked the end of a war of attrition between environmentalists and property developers that had been going on for a quarter of a century. Both the European Union and UNESCO have since recognised Ses Salines as worthy of special protection.

Origins

It was the Phoenicians who first saw the possibility of extracting salt from the coastal lagoons on either side of the Els Freus channel between Ibiza and Formentera. The export of 'white gold', used mainly for preserving meat (especially on board ship), proved to be so lucrative that the Romans and Moors had no hesitation in following suit. After the Catalan invasion in the 13th century, Jaume I allowed the islanders to exploit the salt pans themselves, and from then on profits from the sale were, in theory at least, divided equally. Extracting the salt was back-breaking work, carried out during the hottest time of the year (July and August) following the harvest. The crust on the surface was broken and the salt cut into blocks, before being transported by mule for shipment from Sal Rossa (later from La Canal). Thousands died from malaria, carried by the mosquitoes that bred in the marshes, while murderous raids by marauding Berber pirates were a constant hazard. To protect the island's priceless industrial asset, Felipe II of Spain ordered the building of watchtowers at Sal Rossa and Ses

Portes, using money from salt exports. At first workers from all over the island were drafted for the salt harvest, but over time a small community of labourers built homes near the pans and, in 1771, Carlos III of Spain allowed them to build their own church, Sant Francesc d'Estany (St Francis of the Salt Pans).

Today

Essentially the industry has changed little over the centuries. Tractors have replaced mules, and cargo vessels have taken the place of sailing boats, but the system of sluice gates, pumps and water channels visitors see today is based on the technology introduced by the Moors in the 11th century. The harvest has fallen in recent years from a high point of around 80,000 tons (72,570 tonnes) to an average of 65,000 tons (58,970 tonnes). In the last wet year (2002), production dropped to a meagre 35,000 tons (31,750 tonnes). Most of the salt is exported to the countries of northern Europe. In Scotland it is used mainly for gritting roads in winter, while the Norwegians and Icelanders use salt for preserving cod.

Opposite: Ses Salines beach
Above: Salt has been a precious commodity since Phoenician times

Walk:
Ses Salines Natural Park

A walk or cycle ride is the best possible introduction to the delights of the Ses Salines Natural Park. The route suggested here is about 12km (7.5 miles) long, but the terrain is mostly flat. However, you can, if you wish, break it up into smaller sections. Buses return to Eivissa from La Canal, Platja den Bossa and Sant Jordi. In the summer you will need a head covering and a supply of water, though you can stock up with food and drink along the way. Bring mosquito repellant in the summer, and especially in September.
Allow 4 hours.

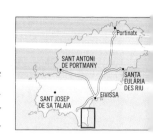

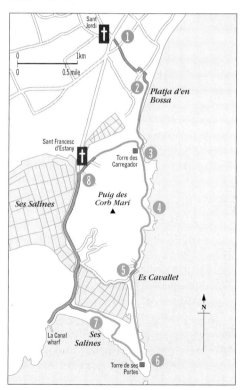

1 Sant Jordi

The church, which looks more like a fortress with its thick, windowless walls and crenellated battlements, is dedicated, appropriately enough, to the dragon-slaying knight, St George. In fact, like most of Ibiza's churches it *was* a fortress, built to protect the local population from pirate attacks.

2 Platja d'en Bossa

The road opposite the church leads from Sant Jordi to Platja d'en Bossa. With 3km (2 miles) of fine, white sand, this is understandably one of the island's more popular beaches, though it's more familiar to clubbers for the dance venues Space and Bora Bora.

3 Torre des Carregador

Head south to the quieter end of the beach where the path crosses an acrid water channel, carrying sea water into the salt marshes. The 16th-century defence tower was built to guard both Eivissa itself and the salt pans. From just below the tower, there are splendid views of Figueretes and, beyond, the walled town of Dalt Vila, crowned by the cathedral.

4 Cliff-top stroll

The path skirts Cala de Sal Rossa ('Red Salt Cove'), then ascends to the cliffs. For the next 4km (2.5 miles) you will be following the shoreline southwards, passing through pine forest and patches of sweet-scented rosemary. At the end you emerge onto Es Cavallet beach by the La Escollera restaurant.

5 Es Cavallet

Ibiza's first designated nudist beach is a vast expanse of pure, dazzling sand,

backed by dunes and pines. If you can, avoid the temptation to linger and continue walking to Punta de ses Portes, the end of the narrow, rocky peninsula that marks the southernmost point of the island.

6 A chain of islands

From the defence tower here (Torre de ses Portes) you get a good view of the lighthouses on the islands of d'es Penjats and des Porcs. Beyond are the two closest islands to Formentera, Espalmador and Espardell. Cormorants sun themselves on the rocks around the point and you may even see the comparatively rare Audouin's gull – look for the red beak.

7 Ses Salines

Follow the path for about 10 minutes, passing a series of miniature coves, and you will come to another superb dune beach known as Ses Salines. At the far end is the La Canal wharf where salt is loaded for export to northern Europe.

8 Sant Francesc d'Estany

Pick up the main 802 road which crosses the glistening pans before skirting a hill called Puig des Corb Marí. Ahead of you is the church of Sant Francesc d'Estany, a chapel built in the 18th century for the salt workers. Just before you get to the church, you'll see a dirt track off to the right. Follow this back to the Torre des Carregador and Platja d'en Bossa.

Platja d'en Bossa is popular with clubbers

Formentera

Lying 16km (10 miles) south of Eivissa, Formentera is the smallest of the Balearic Islands, with an area of 84sq km (32sq miles) and a permanent population of around 5,000. Most of the terrain is flat, with the exception of the Cap de Barbària plateau in the south and the pine-forested hills of La Mola to the east, the highest point being Sa Talaiassa (202m (663ft)). Nowadays, Formentera's residents earn their livelihood from tourism, although the islanders are still proud of their time-honoured customs and traditions, observed with special panache during the patronal festivals held in all the major villages.

Fishing boat at Es Caló de Sant Agustí

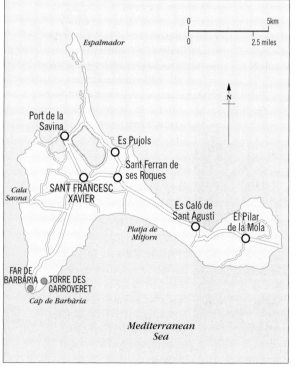

Most visitors to Formentera are day trippers, but an increasing number are tempted to spend more time here because of the beauty of the countryside – still largely unspoilt – and the fabulous beaches. To protect the environment, visitors are asked to explore the island on foot or by bicycle, though there is a bus service connecting the main villages and resorts. The tourist office in La Savina has brochures with suggested walking and cycling routes. This is also the place to ask about guided tours of Formentera's salt marshes, part of the Ses Salines Natural Park. Swimming,

View north to Ibiza from Formentera

water-skiing, windsurfing, canoeing on the Estany des Peix lagoon, rod or underwater fishing, and birdwatching are among the other activities available.

Some history

People were living on Formentera more than 4,000 years ago, and evidence of their activities has been discovered at three prehistoric sites, Cap de Barbària, Can na Costa and Sa Cala. The Romans farmed the land so successfully that they called it *Frumentaria* ('island of wheat'). They established a port in the natural harbour of Caló de Sant Agustí and built a military encampment to guard the approaches. After the Romans departed, the island was invaded by the Vandals, the Byzantines, the Arabs and the Normans, though there is no evidence that any of them settled here for any length of time. The situation changed after the Catalan conquest. Like Ibiza, Formentera was divided into *quartons*

for administrative purposes and recolonised. Within a century, however, pirate raids and the ravages of the Black Death put paid to these plans, and the few islanders who remained were left to fend for themselves. It was not until 1697 that Carlos II of Spain entrusted the sea captain, Marc Ferrer, with the task of supervising the resettlement of the island, which took off surprisingly quickly after Formentera's defences were strengthened with a ring of new watch-towers. So successful was the repopulation that by the middle of the 19th century the island was unable to sustain the growing number of inhabitants, many of whom emigrated to Central and South America. Formentera's economy was saved by the timely arrival of the tourist boom in the 1970s, heralded by the hippies.

BIRDWATCHING

The Cap de Barbària is a great location for birdwatching. It is the first stop on the route from North Africa for migrating species such as the spotted flycatcher, woodchat shrike and nightingale, and a breeding site for the blue rock thrush, Thekla lark and red-legged partridge that nest among the rocks and rosemary bushes. Swooping around the headland itself are Balearic shearwaters, Audouin's gulls and peregrine falcons.

Barbària Peninsula

As one contemplates the increasingly arid landscape along the road south from Sant Francesc, it seems difficult to imagine this as the site chosen by the island's first settlers. Yet the evidence suggests a sizeable megalithic community, making a living from raising livestock and rudimentary crop growing. There is no natural water source on the island, so the settlers must have collected rainwater in wells, as their descendants continued to do through the centuries, until the building of a desalination plant in recent times. The construction methods they used are similar to those of the Talayotic peoples of Mallorca and Menorca, suggesting possible trading links. Three sites have been excavated. Barbària II and III would have been living quarters, stables and workshops, while Barbària I is thought to have been a place of worship. All three sites are just off the main road

and easy to locate. The name Barbària recalls the Barbary Coast of North Africa (little more than 100km (62 miles) to the south) and the pirates who were the bane of the islanders for centuries. The 18th-century watchtower known as the **Torre des Garroveret** (to the left of the main road, just beyond the megalithic settlement) is a reminder of those troubled times. Overlooking the cliffs at the cape, almost 80m (263ft) above sea level, is the **Barbària Lighthouse** (**Far de Barbària**) – next stop Algeria!

Ca na Costa

(*See p90*)

Castell Romà de Can Blai

A turn-off near the 10km (6 mile) marker on the road from Sant Francesc leads to the remains of a Roman fort (*castellum*), thought to date from the 3rd century AD. One can make out the

Land's end at Cap de Barbària

Platja de Migjorn offers great facilities for beach lovers

foundations of the perimeter wall and the bases of five rectangular towers, though little else. The encampment at Can Blai guarded the Camí Romà, then the most important road on the island, and the approaches to the port of Es Calò de Sant Agustí (*see p126*).

Platja de Arenal de Migjorn

This stunning beach, one of the finest in the Pitiusas, begins 2.5km (1.5 miles) east of Sant Ferran (take the side turning to Es Ca Marí). Arrive here and, stretching before you for the next 6km (4 miles), is an almost unbroken vista of dazzling white sand, dunes and pines. Conveniently sited at the back of the beach are half a dozen excellent *chiringuitos* serving snacks and cold

drinks. You could also check out the famous Blue Bar. Perched on a hillock to the west of Es Ca Marí is the **Torre de Migjorn** (also known as Torre des pi des Català), a watchtower which last saw action in 1813 when a party of French soldiers tried to land here but was repulsed. A little further along the coast is an idyllic little spot called **Es Torrent de s'Alga** where the local fishermen mend their nets and lay out their catch in the sun to dry. The countryside behind the beach is typical of Formentera's central isthmus – wheat fields enclosed by drystone walls, fig trees, prickly pears (thought to discourage mosquitoes) and whitewashed houses, the trailing bougainvillea adding an extra dash of colour.

Snorkelling is a popular pursuit at Es Calò de Sant Agustí

Es Calò de Sant Agustí

The northern coast of Formentera is much rockier than the south – windier, too. Nevertheless, there are some attractive spots here, among them Es Calò. The monks from the Augustinian monastery in La Mola used to moor their boats here in the 13th century, hence the name. The tiny cove, no more than 30m (98ft) wide, has been a port since Roman times and is still used by fishermen, although wood, coal and sandstone are no longer shipped to Eivissa and the Spanish mainland as they were in the 1920s. The beach is rocky and better suited to snorkelling than swimming, but the fish restaurants, with terraces overlooking the bay, are worth a look. Otherwise, track back along the coast to the beach at **Ses**

Platgetes – much sandier and three times as wide. Alternatively, take the track (Camí Romà) from Es Calò up the hill to **Es Mirador** 1km (0.6 mile) from where there are wonderful panoramic views.

Espalmador

Espalmador is the largest of the islands off the coast of Formentera, privately owned but open to the public. The main attraction is the beach at **Platja des S'Alga**, popular with nudists (though not exclusively). The shallow waters are ideal for swimming and you can improve your skin tone by wallowing in the nearby mud baths. To escape the crowds in July and August, head around the coast to a pair of rocky coves known as **Cala de Bocs**. For centuries,

Espalmador was populated exclusively by goats, but the island's strategic location put it in the front line of defence against the pirates – there was a permanent garrison here of around 50 soldiers. You can still visit the defence tower at **Sa Guadiola**, though you will not be able to see inside. There are excursions to Espalmador from La Savina during the summer.

Es Pujols

Four kilometres (2.5 miles) southeast of La Savina, Es Pujols is the island's main resort, founded at the beginning of the tourist boom in the 1970s but saved from unsightly over-development when

buildings of more than four storeys were outlawed. Behind the pristine beach of white sand is Avda Miramar, a small promenade lined with fairly low-key bars and restaurants, serving everything from pizzas to fresh fish. There is more of the same on the high street, Passeig des Palmeres. Es Pujols is also handy for shops, with a mini-supermarket or two, and several cash points. Last but not least, it boasts Formentera's only dance club, Flower Power (*see p157*). The hinterland of Es Pujols is a wine-growing area, and you can see the vineyards if you take the *Camí de ses Vinyes* Green Route out of the resort towards Sant Ferran.

The pristine white sand and promenade of Es Pujols beach

Cycle Ride: Es Trucadors and Around

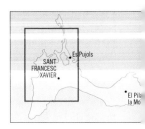

The best way to get around Formentera is to cycle. The terrain is mostly flat, the climate mild, and the views stunning, while the island is criss-crossed by untarmacked tracks and bridle paths, not well-suited to cars. This route explores the north-western reaches of Formentera. It begins at the small resort of Es Pujols, taking in the beaches of the Trucador Peninsula before passing through the sparsely inhabited terrain of the west coast, where clumps of rosemary bushes, drystone walls and stunning sea vistas are the order of the day. The complete circuit is about 28km (17 miles) (12km (7.5 miles) round Estany Pudent and a further 16km (10 miles) to Cala Saona and back).

Allow 3 hours.

1 Ca na Costa

Take the Ses Salines road north from Es Pujols, passing a track on your left that leads to the stone circle at Ca na Costa, the remains of a megalithic burial ground. The 2-m (7-ft) high slabs are an important archaeological find as they were erected by Formentera's earliest settlers.

2 Ses Salines

Continue to Ses Salines and enjoy the natural beauty of Formentera's salt pans, a conservation area since the salt works closed down in 1984.

3 The Trucador Peninsula

Take the right fork at the pans and follow the track which leads to the tapering peninsula of Es Trucadors. After passing the windmill at Moli des Carregedor (now a restaurant), the path continues through a delightful dune and pine landscape revealing the stunning back-to-back beaches of Platja Levant and Platja Illetes – a tempting point to dismount for a cooling swim.

Cycling around the Trucador Peninsula

4 Estany Pudent

Leave the peninsula by the same path, but before reaching the main road take the unpaved track to the right. This route, with the sea on one side and the lagoon on the other, was once followed by the industrial train transporting salt to the dock at La Savina. As the track enters the port, turn left to rejoin the road. After about 500m (0.3 mile), take the next left which skirts the brackish saltwater lake of Estany Pudent. This is a popular spot for birdwatching – look out for herons, egrets, and possibly even a flamingo or two.

5 Sant Francesc Xavier

At the southern point of the lake, follow the signs to the right and you will eventually join the main road. Turn right again for Sant Francesc Xavier, Formentera's tiny capital. Take a short break in the sleepy village square before taking the road to Es Molins de Sa Mirada.

6 Cala Saona

As the road climbs the small hill to the Sa Mirada windmill there are superb views back towards the lakes and the village. Continue to the end of the paved road, then take the track to the left. Follow the marked 'green route' south for 2.5km (1.5 miles) to Cala Saona.

By now you may feel the need for another refreshing dip and this sheltered bay provides the perfect backdrop.

7 Cami de Ses Vinyes

Take the paved road back to Sant Francesc Xavier. Leave the village in the direction of Sant Ferran and you can choose one of two routes back to Es Pujols. The first (about 750m (0.5 mile) from the town) follows a track along the edge of the lagoon. Alternatively, turn left into Sant Ferran, looking out for the first unpaved road on your left. This is known locally as the Cami de Ses Vinyes because it passes through an area of vineyards.

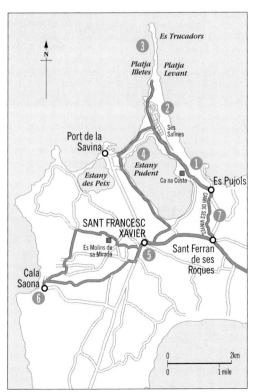

The brackish waters of Estany Pudent are the habitat of numerous marine birds

Estany des Peix

This shallow saltwater lagoon is connected to the sea by a narrow strait through which only very small craft can pass. Because it is closer to the sea than Estany Pudent (*see below*) it attracts gulls, terns and other sea birds. While the salinity level is not particularly high, it is enough for rushes, glasswort and other marsh plants of the *salicornia* genus to thrive. Centuries ago there was a small fishing port here, hence the name 'peix'. Near the road are the remnants of a prisoner-of-war camp where Republican soldiers were held following the end of the Civil War. A signposted Green Route skirts the perimeter of the lagoon with panoramic views across La Savina towards the Es Freus strait.

Estany Pudent

This brackish lagoon only lives up to its name (meaning stagnant) on hot summer days when the sea is at low tide. The fetid conditions, produced by decomposing algae, are exacerbated by accumulations of rainwater, attracting swarms of mosquitoes. Salt concentration is high, three times that of the sea in places, although, surprisingly, some freshwater plants grow here, as well as the more predictable *salcornias* – rushes, giant reeds and sea violets. Flocks of several thousand black-crested grebe have been seen wintering on Estany Pudent, while the reed beds at the southern end of the lagoon attract little ringed and Kentish plovers, spotted redshank, great reed warblers and black-winged stilt. Estany Pudent was originally called 'Flamingo lagoon', and a colony of these beautiful birds still breeds here, although numbers are said to be decreasing.

Outlying islands

Ibiza is separated from Formentera by the **Es Freus** channel. The scattered islands and the waters themselves together form part of the Ses Salines conservation area. Es Freus attracts numerous varieties of sea birds. Colonies of storm petrel, Audouin's and yellow-legged gulls and Balearic shearwater are now established on some of the islands, while fisher eagles and cormorants are also common around these waters. The first of the islets, just beyond the salt pans at Ses Salines, is **Illa d'es Penjats** (Island of the Hanged). The first prisoners to be executed here in 1271 were captured Berber pirates. To the west are the two tiny islands of **Illes Negres** (Black Islands), and beyond them, **Espalmador** (*see p126*). Off the coast of Espalmador are the islands of **Illa des Porcs** (Pig Island), which merits its own lighthouse – the channel can be particularly treacherous here – and **Illa des Torretes** (Turret Island), a reference to earlier defensive functions. Private yachts sometimes moor here, as there are good beaches. On the far side of Espalmador is **Espardell**. Goats pastured here in the past, only to be driven away by the harsh climate, but the rabbits proved to be made of sterner stuff. The endemic Pitiusan wall lizard breeds on Espardell and the island also supports a colony of cormorants.

Illa d'es Penjats' idyllic setting belies the fact that it was once a place of execution

Pilar de la Mola

The pine-wooded ascent from the Mar i Land end of Es Migjorn beach may be tough going but it is worth the effort for the spectacular views of Formentera and the south coast of Ibiza from **Es Mirador**. (Those with foresight will have booked a table on the terrace of the El Mirador restaurant just off the main road.) In fact, the *mirador* is not the highest point on the island – that honour belongs to Sa Talaiassa 202m (663ft), a little further to the east. Just beyond the hill is the plain of La Mola, where the fertile soil nurtures vines, wheat, figs, vegetables and other crops.

The Augustinian monks who cleared the first tract of forest here back in the 13th century began this farming tradition, before falling victim to the Black Death. The hamlet of **El Pilar de la Mola** consists of little more than a few dozen houses clustering round a typical whitewashed parish church (1796). A congenial spot to linger over a drink, El Pilar comes into its own on Sunday-afternoon for the craft market. Going after something authentic may be a wasted exercise, although there are local artisans from the hippie era still at work around here. One or two of them may remember the folk singer Bob Dylan,

Hippies, including it is said Bob Dylan, once inhabited the windmills at El Pilar de la Mola

La Mola – lighthouse at the end of the world

who lived on Formentera for a while in the 1960s. There is a tradition that he set up home in the old windmill (Molí Vell) near the village, which dates from 1778 and is still in working order. From here the Sant Francesc road runs as straight as a die over the final 2km (1.25 miles) to **Far de la Mola**. This was the island's only lighthouse until Cap de Barbària was installed in the early 1970s, and in 1877 it provided the inspiration for the French science fiction writer Jules Verne's novel *Héctor Servadac*. A granite monument reminds visitors of the fact. Rock sparrows find the barren terrain here congenial, while peregrine falcons make their nests in the cliffs. Fortunately, collectors no longer raid the ledges for birds' eggs – this was once such a common practice that it even gave rise to a verb, *virotar*, from the Eivissenc word *virot* (shearwater). South

of Far de la Mola is Es Condolar, a small cove from where supplies of petrol would have been brought up to the lighthouse keeper – a practice which died out less than 50 years ago. To explore the south coast of the island from La Mola, pick up the Camí des Estufador at El Pilar de la Mola, which ends in a steep descent to **S'Estufador**. Along the way are the charcoal stacks (*estufas*) and lime kilns which give the place its name.

Punta de Sa Gavina

A small country road from Estany des Peix leads to the headland of Punta de Sa Gavina, from where there are marvellous views across the island to Espalmador La Savina and the salt lagoons. A watchtower, **Torre de Sa Gavina**, was erected here in the 18th century but never fitted with artillery.

Cycle Ride: To La Mola

The following itinerary, from Sant Francesc Xavier to the eastern tip of the island, is about 15km (9 miles) one way and involves a steep climb to the thickly forested promontory of La Mola. As with the previous itinerary, it is designed with cyclists in mind and incorporates several of the suggested 'green routes'.

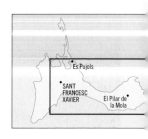

Allow about 3.5 hours without any stops.

1 Isthmus

Leave Sant Francesc Xavier on Calle Sant Jaume, by the Ethnology Museum. At the edge of the town where the road divides, take the right fork. This is part of the old road that runs through the centre of the low, sandy isthmus to the east of the peninsula. It follows a parallel course to the main road which you join after passing the remains of a 3rd-century Roman camp at Can Pins (now no more than a heap of stones). After 1km take the track to the right through wheat fields which give way to pine trees and sand dunes as you approach Platja de Migjorn.

2 Platja de Migjorn

This sweeping crescent of dazzling white sand is characteristic of Formentera's unspoilt beaches. If you have worked up a thirst, there are a handful of excellent *chiringuitos* to choose from.

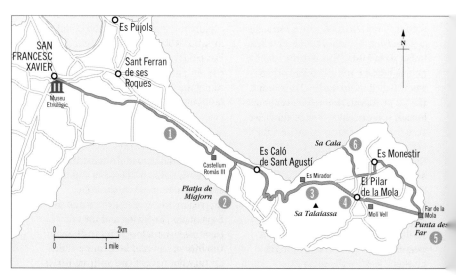

Restaurant Mirador near El Pilar de la Mola

3 Sa Talaiassa

Take any of the paths from the beach to return to the main road. Continue past the small fishing port of Es Caló de San Agustí and begin the climb to the plateau. Sa Talaiassa, the highest point on the island at over 200m (656ft), is off to your right. This is a tough 1.5-km (1-mile) ride, but the *mirador* at the 14km (9 miles) marker makes it worth the effort. As you stop to recover your breath, you can enjoy wonderful views across the bay of Sant Agustí and the isthmus.

4 El Pilar de la Mola

The road now descends to the tiny village of El Pilar de la Mola, which becomes surprisingly busy on Wednesday and Sunday evenings (summer only), when a small craft market is held in the square.

5 Punta Roja

Continue along the main road past the 18th-century Molí Vell, an old windmill still in working order. Three kilometres (2 miles) further on is Far de la Mola, a 102-m (335-ft) tall lighthouse which stands at the eastern tip of the island. Nearby is a monument to the French writer, Jules Verne, who immortalised this 'lighthouse at the end of the world' in his book *Héctor Servadac.*

6 Sa Cala

If you have the time and are not too exhausted, take the right-hand track across the cliffs to Es Monestir, named after a 13th-century Augustinian monastery that was abandoned at the time of the Black Death (1348). Continue through agricultural land to the cliffs at Sa Cala, from where there are superb views of the north coastline.

Sant Ferran, Formentera's second town

you set out on holiday. Some ageing hippies still live in the area, eking out a living selling paintings and knick-knacks outside the church or on the square.

Sant Francesc Xavier

About 2km (1.25 miles) from La Savina, the tiny island 'capital' (population 1,000) is a useful port of call if you need to use a post office, pharmacy or bank, but only worth a quick visit otherwise. Opposite the town hall on the main square is the **Church of Sant Francesc**. Built between 1726 and 1738, it was fortified with cannon at one time, a necessary precaution as pirates were a menace as late as the middle of the 19th century. There is little to see inside, apart from a curious baptismal font by the main door. It predates the church by up to a thousand years but its origins are shrouded in mystery. At a push one can make out oxen's heads and a human face among the faded sculptures. The battered little community which lived here in the Middle Ages worshipped in the **Capella de sa Tanca**. Built in the 14th century, it fell into disuse not long afterwards when the Black Death more or less finished off the island's beleaguered population. New colonists, arriving on Formentera at the end of the 17th century, restored the building, though it is so tiny that only a few of them would have been able to attend services. The most interesting exhibit in

Sant Ferran

Sant Ferran de ses Roques, to give the village its full title, used to be closer to the salt lagoons where most of the population made its living, but when the church fell into disrepair in the 1870s it was decided to relocate a little further inland. Most tourists make a beeline for **Can Pepe**, a bar that has nostalgic associations for hippies – the folk singer Bob Dylan stayed there at one time. Mementoes of the era cover the walls, and such is the cachet of the place that you need to book a room long before

the **Ethnology Museum** (**Museu Etnològic**) – the diminutive steam engine which hauled salt to the dock at La Savina – is outside. If a sandy cove, sheltered from the wind by a pine-forested headland, sounds an attractive proposition at this point, cycle the 2.5-km (1.5-mile) Green Route to **Cala Saona**. More scenic than the main road, it also cuts the journey time in half. It is hard to credit, but a 16th-century map depicts a busy port at Cala Saona with anchorage for 400 ships. Earlier still, the falcons which bred on the cliffs were trained here for hunting.

Ethnology Museum. Open: Mon–Sat 10am–1.30pm.

Pretty as a picture – Plaça de sa Constitució, the main square in Sant Francesc Xavier

Sa Savina

Today, Formentera has only one port of entry, Sa (sometimes La) Savina. An island until the breakwater was constructed in the 1930s, the harbour was widened to accommodate cruise ships from Mallorca and the mainland. Ferries from Ibiza disembark at the quayside near the first of two yachting marinas where you will also find the offices of diving schools and boat hire firms. Fishing trips are advertised and there are numerous bike rental outlets all offering reasonable rates. Hire a mountain bike if you aim to get as far as La Mola or the Barbària peninsula. The shops stay open until the last ferry has sailed so there is no rush to return bikes.

The best of the local restaurants is Aigüa on the quayside but Sa Savina offers little else to detain the visitor. Buses to Sant Francesc, Sant Ferran, Es Pujols and La Mola depart from the stop near the tourist information office. There is a taxi rank here, too.

Trucador peninsula

Hyperbole aside, the 3-km (2-mile) spur extending to the northernmost point of Formentera deserves the description of Mediterranean paradise. Boat excursions to Espalmador from La Savina call at Ses Illetes, but the extraordinary beauty of Es Trucadors is best discovered on a bike. Follow the Camí de Ses Illetes around the Estany Pudent lagoon, then

Harbour at Sa Savina is a hive of activity

take the signposted turning. Along the way are sublime views across the dunes, pines and salt pans which form part of the Ses Salines Natural Park, one of the most ecologically diverse regions in the Mediterranean. The road leads to the car park and a choice of two pristine beaches, equally devoid of urban development. On the western side of the promontory is **Ses Illetes** which takes its name from the offshore islands of Pouet and Rodona – close enough to swim to if the sea is calm – while to the east is **Platja de Llevant**. As the distance between the two is never more than 200m (656ft) it's possible to 'beach hop'. This idea isn't as crazy as it sounds because, owing to a quirk of nature, the onshore breezes affect only one side of the promontory at a time. While Es Trucadors is a popular destination at the

height of the summer, it's always possible to find a space. *Chiringuitos* are placed strategically along the beaches and are better value than the local restaurants. Anyone in a more adventurous frame of mind will find that water-skiing, hang-gliding and other sports are available. Having got this far you may be tempted to reconnoitre the last stretch of the peninsula, but to do this you will have to leave the bikes behind. The track peters out at **Es Pas des Trucadors**, the straits separating Formentera from the island of S'Espalmador. The hardy plant which grows in the shallow water here (*herba des Trucadors*) is said to be good for curing stomach aches. The dunes are more fragile, sometimes disappearing altogether when overlapped by the incoming tide.

Outside the high season Ses Illetes is all but deserted

Palma, Mallorca

A visit to one of the other Balearic islands (in this case, Mallorca) not only provides a change of scene, but is an opportunity to discover the subtle differences between two Catalan cultures. Mallorca's capital is a lively city with a population of 300,000, ten times that of Eivissa.

Juggler at Plaça Major, Palma

There is a great deal to see, including a magnificent harbour, a glorious mediaeval cathedral, a Moorish castle, a ruined Arab baths and a collection of superb aristocratic mansions dating from the 15th to the 19th centuries. Palma has a sophisticated cosmopolitan air and among its other attractions are excellent shopping and nightlife. There are tourist offices at Carrer Santo Domingo 11 and Caseta Plaça Espanya.

LA SEU (CATHEDRAL)

One of the jewels of Spanish Gothic architecture, work on Palma's pinnacled cathedral was begun in the 13th century, shortly after the Christian Reconquest. The building was restored in the early 1900s by the great Catalan architect, Antoni Gaudí. Special points of interest include the stunning stained glass (the cathedral boasts the largest rose window in the world), the wrought-iron baldachino by Gaudí above the main altar and the cathedral museum with its displays of precious religious objects and Gothic art works.
Plaça d'Almoina. Open: Apr–Oct, Mon–Fri 10am–6pm, Sat 10am–2pm; Nov–Mar, Mon–Fri 10am–3pm, Sat 10am–2pm. Admission charge.

PALAU DE L'ALMUDAINA

This imposing building was originally the palace of the Moorish governors of the city and was subsequently adapted for use by the Christian rulers of Mallorca. It is still one of the official residences of the king and queen of Spain. The remains of the **Banys Arabs** (**Arab Baths**), lost in the picturesque warren of streets behind the cathedral, are another reminder of the Moorish presence in the city.
Palace, Carrer Palau Reial.
Tel: (971) 72 71 45. Open for guided tours Apr–Sept, Mon–Fri 10am–6pm, Sat 10am–2pm; Oct–Mar, Mon–Fri 10am–2pm, 4–6pm. Admission charge.
Arab Baths, Carrer Can Serra.
Tel: (971) 72 15 49. Open: daily 9am–8pm. Admission charge.

FUNDACIÓ PILAR I JOAN MIRÓ

The home and purpose-built studio of one of Spain's most innovative modern artists contains more than 100 of his paintings, as well as sculptures and other works.
Carrer Joan de Saridakis 29, Cala Major.
Tel: (971) 70 14 20. Open: 15 May–15 Sept, Tue–Sat 10am–7pm, Sun 10am–5pm; 16 Sept–14 May, Tue–Sat 10am–6pm, Sun 10am–3pm.

Palma Cathedral soars above the harbour

A visit to the Spanish Mainland

Ibiza has a Spanish as well as a Catalan flavour, mainly due to the large influx of workers from the mainland in the 1960s and 1970s. You can even see the coastline (on a clear day, at least) from one or two points on the island, so the temptation to visit may prove irresistible. There are direct sailings to Valencia and Denia – the Denia option includes the possibility of an onward coach connection to Valencia.

The Trasmediterránea ferry makes regular trips to Valencia

DENIA

This bustling port has a rich history and culture dating back to Carthaginian times. Near the port is a delightful old quarter of cobbled streets and trim, whitewashed buildings. The main sight, the 16th-century castle, dominates the town. Denia has some great tapas bars and seafood restaurants on the waterfront and the cafés on the main street, Calle Marques de Campo, are also worth checking out. The Costa de Alzahar is a region of beautiful beaches, mostly blue flag. An alternative to Denia itself is the charming resort of Jávea (easily reached by taxi). The sands here were immortalised in the work of the Spanish artist Joaquín Sorolla at the beginning of the 20th century, and the attractive hillside village merits a look. Denia's tourist information office is on Calle Patricio Ferrandiz.
Tel: (965) 57 80 957.

VALENCIA

Spain's third largest city (population 800,000) is a thriving port, renowned for its nightlife. Its history dates back to

Roman times, and there is a great deal to see in and around the crumbling **Barrio del Carmen**. The most arresting Gothic monument is the beautifully proportioned **Silk Exchange** (Lonja de los Mercaderes). There are wonderful views of the city from the roof of Valencia's **Cathedral**, also medieval in origin. The huge glass and wrought-iron **Central Market** (Mercado Central) is one of the largest in Europe and showcases Spain's most productive market garden region. Also worth a look is the **Fine Arts Museum** (Museu de Belles Artes), with works by El Greco, Hieronymus Bosch, Velázquez and Goya, and the spanking new **City of Arts and Sciences** (Ciudad de las Artes y las Ciencias), a major architectural landmark, built to house an arts centre, cinemas, a planetarium, and the largest aquarium in Europe (Parque Oceanográfico). Cafés and restaurants abound in the streets to the south of the cathedral. Valencia is the home of the rice-based dish, paella, but you should also try *fideúa* (a mixture of seafood and noodles cooked paella style). In the summer the refreshing non-alcoholic drink, *horchata*, made from tiger nuts and best served *granizada* (with ice), is an excellent thirst quencher. The Tourist Information office is on Plaza del Ayuntamiento. *Tel: (963) 51 04 17.*

The castle, the first sight to greet visitors approaching Denia harbour

PRACTICALITIES
Getting to Palma, Mallorca
Trasmediterránea High-speed ferries depart from Eivissa for Palma Tuesday to Sunday at 8pm (journey time 2 hours). Ferries from Palma returning to Eivissa depart at 7.45am.
Tel: (971) 31 51 00.
www.trasmediterranea.es
Balearia This company operates two services. The slow ferry leaves Eivissa at 1.15pm daily and takes 4.5 hours. The fast service (2 hours) departs at 8pm, Monday to Saturday. Return services from Palma are (slow) daily at 9.30am and (fast) at 8am, Sunday to Friday.
Tel: (971) 31 40 05. www.balearia.com

Realistically, visiting Palma from Ibiza involves a stay of a couple of nights.

ACCOMMODATION
Hostal Born **
Refurbished mansion with a courtyard café in a good central location. Book in advance.
Carrer Sant Jaume 3, Palma.
Tel: (971) 71 29 42.

Convent de la Missió ***
Acclaimed in the Spanish press, this hotel opened in 2003 in a restored 17th-century convent built for missionary priests. The striking modernist interiors were designed by Rafael Balaguer and Antoni Esteva. Book in advance.
Carrer de la Missió 7, Palma.
Tel: (971) 22 73 47.
www.conventdelamissio.com

Terrace restaurants are a Spanish institution

GETTING TO MAINLAND SPAIN

Trasmediterránea The high-speed ferry leaves Eivissa for Valencia at 10.30am Tuesday to Sunday and takes 3 hours. Ferries from Valencia to Eivissa depart at 4.30pm.
Tel: (902) 45 46 45 (Valencia) or (971) 31 51 00 (Ibiza).
www.trasmediterranea.es

Balearia The fast ferry to Denia leaves Eivissa at 11am Sunday to Friday and arrives 2 hours later. The coach connection from Denia to Valencia takes an extra 1 hour 15 minutes. The slow ferry departs at 2.15pm daily and takes 4 hours to reach Denia. Again allow an extra 1 hour 15 minutes for the onward journey to Valencia. Ferries from Denia returning to Eivissa depart at

5pm Monday to Saturday (fast) and at 8.30pm daily (slow).
Tel: (971) 31 40 05. www.balearia.com
The trip to Denia could be done as a day excursion, but the Valencia extension necessitates an overnight stay.

ACCOMMODATION
Hotel Costa Blanca **

Modern hotel with an ideal location only 50m from the quayside, yet equally convenient for the shopping and tourist areas.
Pintor Llorens 3, Denia. Tel: (965) 780 336.

Hotel Venecia **

Excellent value, this hotel is handily situated for exploring the historic sights in the city. Highly recommended.
Plaza Ayuntamiento (entrance on Calle En Llop 5), Valencia. Tel: (963) 524 267.

The old centre of Valencia is an engaging mix of architectural styles

Shopping

Since the euro was introduced in January 2002 retail prices have risen sharply in Spain, more sharply in fact than in any other country in 'Euroland', with the exception of Ireland. Now for the good news: while books, DVDs, personal stereos, computers and kitchen equipment are more expensive than in northern Europe, most other items, including clothes, shoes, CDs and a lot of foodstuffs, are still competitively priced. Most tourist shops offer tax-free shopping for non-EU residents. In cases where IVA (Value Added Tax) is applicable, it will be levied at between 9 and 17 per cent, depending on the purchase.

Precision artist at work

What to buy

A creation of the 1970s, the Ad Lib 'look' is again the height of Spanish chic and gaining international attention on the fashion circuit. Traditional handicrafts have taken a bit of a pummelling from foreign competition, but if you look hard enough you can still find genuine, high-quality pottery and ceramics, embroidery, basket weaving, tapestries, leather goods, *espardenyes* (espadrilles or grass sandals), traditional folk instruments and the local liqueur, *Hierbas Ibicencas*. During the summer, craft fairs and markets are held at various locations around the islands – look out for advertisements or check with the nearest tourist office for details.

Where to shop

In Eivissa, head to Dalt Vila for Ad Lib clothing and accessories, antiques and modern art. The clothing stores and boutiques of La Marina and Sa Penya (especially on Carrer Mare de Déu and Carrer Major) also stock Ad Lib fashions and are an excellent source for clubbing outfits. For general shopping, start with

---

AD LIB

This uniquely Ibizan fashion phenomenon took off in the early 1970s, a few years after Smilja Mijailovich, a Serb-born princess, had opened the first clothing store with the Ad Lib label (from the Latin *ad libitum*, meaning 'anything goes'). Drawing her inspiration from traditional folk costumes and the 'dressing-down' styles of Ibizan hippies, she and her fellow designers combined plain white fabrics such as cotton and calico with bright colours. The Ibiza 'look', also characterised by revealing, flouncy bodices, low-slung leather belts and wooden sandals, has enjoyed a new lease of life, thanks to the interest of fashion-conscious celebrities like Claudia Schiffer and Penelope Cruz.

Passeig Vara del Rey then move on to the busy streets of the new town, especially Bartolomeu Rosselló, Isidor Macabich and Ignasi Wallis. This is where the locals shop, so prices are more competitive than in the tourist areas.

Art and antiques

While you're unlikely to find genuine antiquities for sale anywhere in the Pitiusas, you will find an interesting assortment of 19th- and 20th-century books, furniture, paintings and curios. The work of dozens of contemporary artists living on the islands is also available and well worth a browse.

Art for sale in Eivissa's Dalt Vila

Carl van der Voort

Exclusive, high quality and expensive, Ibiza's leading art gallery has been run by this fine-art consultant since 1966. Twentieth-century and contemporary paintings, sculptures and original prints. *Plaça de la Vila 13, Dalt Vila, Eivissa.*

Casi Todo

Sales take place monthly (sometimes twice monthly) at this English-owned auction house, where you can find everything from vintage motorbikes to grandfather clocks. *Santa Gertrudis.*

Bookshops

Lavish art or coffee-table books are, on the whole, more expensive here than in northern Europe, although there is the occasional bargain to be had. Books on Ibiza and Formentera abound and make good souvenirs. Several bookstores have foreign-language sections for anyone missing a good read.

Casa Azul

Stocks a comprehensive range of books on Ibiza and Formentera. Also specialises in architecture and design, photography and culture. And there's a café on the premises. *Carrer Caleta Soler 9, New Town, Eivissa. Also Santa Gertrudis.*

Window shopping in Eivissa's La Marina district

Island Books
British-owned bookstore with extensive range of fiction, travel, Ibizan and Spanish titles. Second-hand department on the first floor.
Carrer d'Osca 8, Santa Eulària.

Clothing and boutiques
Arizona
Exclusive, made-to-measure, quality leather fashions from a workshop founded in 1983.
Avda Andenes s/n, Sa Penya, Eivissa.
Tel: (971) 31 09 19.

Boutique Divina
Ad Lib *haute couture* for men, women and children, at prices to match.
Carrer Santa Creu s/n, Dalt Vila, Eivissa.

Can Felix
Motley selection of traditional and modern fans, costumes and beaded shawls at affordable prices.
Carrer Antoni Palau 1, La Marina, Eivissa.

Cantonada
One of the longest-established Ad Lib outlets on the island. Off-the-peg day and evening wear in natural fabrics and light or warm colours.
Carrer Comte de Rosselló 10, New Town, Eivissa.

Funkin' Irie
Next to the Azul bookstore, this boutique caters especially for clubbers (male and female), with a suitably provocative range of outfits and accessories. You can shop here for vinyl and CDs too.
Carrer Caleta Soler 7, New Town, Eivissa.

Ibiza Republic Boutique
Designer Bernadette Loriot's store is the height of Ibiza cool. Shop here for tops, dresses, wraps, swimwear, jogging gear and sandals. English-speaking staff.
Carrer Antoni-Mari 15, Eivissa.
Tel: (971) 31 41 75.

Marta Raffo
For a highly individual take on Ad Lib fashions.
Carrer de Mere de Déu 63, Sa Penya, Eivissa.

Sandal Shop
Everything for the leather enthusiast – handmade bags, belts, sandals, boots – though at a price.
Plaça de la Vila s/n.

Te Cuero
All kinds of leather goods, but mainly handbags and accessories.
Santa Gertrudis.

Food and drink
When you've done shopping for Ibizan liqueurs, pause to investigate the spirits and Spanish wines. The prices will bowl you over.

Bodega Ribas
Second-generation business specialising in quality Spanish wines and liqueurs (including *Hierbas Ibicencas*). Also a selection of champagnes, all at competitive prices.
Carrer Sant Vicent (just off Plaça Espanya), Santa Eulària.
Tel: (971) 33 19 90.

Casa Alfonso
Useful downtown off-licence with excellent deli section.
Corner of Sant Antoni and Carrer Ample

(behind Marina), *Sant Antoni.*
Tel: (971) 34 05 10.

Ecolandia
Everything you need for healthy eating. This health-food supermarket and café-restaurant has an extensive selection of organic fruit and vegetables, wine, beer, cereals, milk, Ibizan honey and fresh bread for sale.
Avda Dr Fleming 37, Sant Antoni.

Marí Mayans
Official outlet of the leading distiller of Ibizan herb liqueurs since 1880. *Hierbas Ibicencas* is flavoured with aniseed, thyme, rosemary, lemon and orange peel but you should also try *Palo* (drunk as an aperitif with a few drops of gin added) and *Frígola*, a drier Ibizan liqueur. Marí Mayans is also renowned for its absinthe.
Carrer V. Marí Mayans 19–21, Puig den Valls, Santa Eulària. Tel: (971) 31 20 13.
Also Eivissa and Sant Antoni.

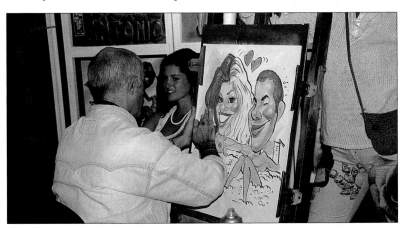

Spitting image? Caricaturist's view of a visitor to Sant Antoni

Records and CDs

As you might expect from Europe's clubbing capital, there are a number of excellent record stores stocking vinyl and CD dance mixes. Start your search at one of the following:

Pacha records
Carrer Lluis Tur I Palau 20, New Town, Eivissa.

Plastic Fantastic
Carrer Sant Antoni 15, Sant Antoni.

Souvenirs
El Paraiso
Lladro porcelain is not to everyone's taste, but if you are a fan you'll find prices considerably lower here than in northern Europe. At the last count, this outlet stocked more than 1,000 figurines, including limited editions. It also sells cut glass.

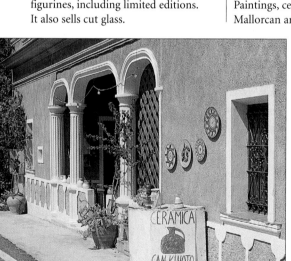

Ceramics are the speciality of Sant Rafel

Carrer M. Riquer Wallis (near the beach), Santa Eulària. Tel: (971) 33 13 16.

Groch
International perfumes at reduced prices, as well as Spanish and even Ibizan fragrances. This retailer also sells bags, belts and other fashion accessories.
Punta Arabí end of Es Canar beach.

Magic crystal
Spaniards are great fans of the occult – there are a number of popular TV shows and phone-in programmes dealing with the subject. This shop stocks crystal balls, incense, purifiers, oracles, books and packs of tarot cards.
Carrer Galicia (street behind the beach), Figueretes.

Torrent Fondo
Paintings, ceramics, leather, crystal, Mallorcan artificial pearls, even toys – you'll find them all here in this store in the centre of town.
Passeig Aljemesi, just off Passeig Alameira, Santa Eulària.

Sports shops
Deportes El Corral
Large sports stockists with a comprehensive range of clothing, shoes and equipment. Leading brand names and latest models at prices to suit every pocket.
Carrer Sant Antoni 23, Sant Antoni.
Tel: (971) 34 05 17.

Attention-grabbing designs are a feature of Ibizan leatherware

holdalls, bags, sandals, CDs and games.
San Jaume, 76, Santa Eulària. Also at Es Canar (Punta Arabí road).

Craft markets

Ibiza is famous for its hippie markets, though you'll be lucky to find much in the way of authentic handicrafts nowadays. If you're on the lookout for a sarong or a tie-dye shirt, on the other hand, look no further.

Eivissa. By the port. *Open daily in summer.*

El Pilar de la Mola, Formentera.
Art market in the central square. Locally made jewellery and handicrafts. *Open May to September, Wednesday and Sunday.*

Platja d'En Bossa. In Bahamas Complex. *Open Fridays in summer.*

Punta Arabi – Es Canar. The best known of the markets. *Open Wednesdays during the summer 10am–7pm.*

Sant Carles – Las Dahlias.
Arguably the best of the bunch. *Open all day Saturday, all year round.*

Sant Jordi. At the hippodrome. Second-hand and hippie market. *Open Saturdays all year.*

Santa Eulària des Riu.
A small line of stalls on the main street, Paseo de la Alameda. *Open all year Monday–Tuesday and Thursday–Saturday.*

Kalani

This surf shop has boards for hire, plus wetsuits, clothing and every other accessory you think you might need.
Carrer del Progrès 34, Sant Antoni.

Holidays

Everything for the water-sports enthusiast, including surfing and scuba-diving gear. Also sporting equipment,

Eivissa's medieval festival

On the second weekend in May, Dalt Vila springs to life with a major festival marking the World Heritage status conferred on the town by UNESCO in 1999. The first celebration took place the following year and now attracts an estimated 100,000 visitors. The aim is to celebrate Eivissa's rich architectural and cultural heritage – part of the proceeds goes to restoration and conservation projects within the walled town. In the days leading up to the festival, Dalt Vila's winding streets echo to the sound of hammer and nails as the stalls (more than a hundred in all) are erected. Meanwhile, volunteers hang bunting, flags and pennants and install flaming torches for the evening events. The show gets underway with a welcome concert from the Musikkapelle Ciutat d'Eivissa (City of Eivissa Music Band). There are around two dozen shows and theatrical events each year,

held in venues all over the town: from Ses Taules and Mercat Vell to the cathedral square and the cloisters of the Town Hall. The theme throughout is Medieval and Renaissance, traditional and esoteric. Past events have included organ recitals, sephardic singing, Arab dancing displays, Commedia dell' Arte and tongue-in-cheek pageants like 'Eivissa against the Grand Turk' or 'Moors versus Christians'. To attract the children there are archery and falconry displays, not to mention donkey rides. When they're not being entertained, visitors can browse the stalls, manned by locals decked out in mediaeval costume. Traditional handicrafts are represented with embroidery, woodwork, ceramics and basket weaving. You can buy decorative candles and joss sticks, jade necklaces, Ibizan liqueurs, aromatic shampoos, medicinal herbs, honey, jam, wines and cheeses – you name it. At supper time spicy sausages are cooked over an open fire and served with bread rolls and a glass of wine or beer. With incomparable views of the harbour from the battlements, what more could anyone wish for? Don't miss it.

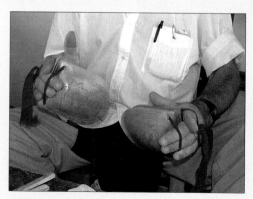

Fiesta Patronal

Dalt Vila's other important summer festival, held from 4–8 August, honours the

city's co-patrons, Our Lady of the Snows (Mare de Déu de les Neus, 5 August) and Sant Ciriac (8 August). The feast of St Ciriac also marks the day when, in 1235, the Arabs were expelled from the city by the Catalans, led by Guillem de Montgrí. In the morning there is a solemn high mass in the cathedral, followed by a procession to San Ciriac's chapel and a folk-dancing exhibition. In the evening everyone heads for Puig des Molins and the traditional *berenada* (supper) of *coca amb pebrera* (pastries with red peppers), buns and watermelons. The highlight is the watermelon fight in Es Soto beneath the city walls. Throughout the festival, the confraternities, called *collas*, put on

shows of traditional village dances (*ball pagès*) to the accompaniment of flutes, drums and castanets. The *Colla de la Vila* performs in front of the cathedral on the evening of 5 August, the *Colla Sa Bodega* at the quayside on the following evening, traditionally the fishermen's day (there's a ceremony at the Monument to the Corsairs). All these festive acts are rounded off with stunning firework displays which illuminate the city walls and the Mediterranean beyond.

Opposite: Playing traditional castanets
Above: Colourful dancing displays are the hallmark of Ibizan festivals

Entertainment

Essentially, entertainment in Ibiza is its bars and nightclubs. These range from terraces with captivating sea views to old hippie haunts, tapas bars, chill-out and beach bars. Most are open all day and until late (at least 1am), some round the clock. The best areas to head for in Eivissa are La Marina and Sa Penya, though Dalt Vila is also worth checking out and, of course, the beaches – especially Platja d'en Bossa – in summer.

Carnival in clubland

The best bars in Sant Antoni are in the area known as 'Sunset Strip' on the way to Caló des Moro. Santa Eulària is not known for its nightlife, but does have one disco-bar, Guaraná. Technically, the clubbing season begins at the beginning of June but actually takes a week or two to get underway. Thereafter it's all go until the end of September. Only two clubs, Pacha and El Divino (both in Eivissa), remain open during winter, when there are substantial price reductions. Space, on Playa d'en Bossa, is open during the day (and sometimes at night). Some clubs and music bars, notably Km 5, have recently been having problems renewing their licences as the local authorities are clamping down on excessive noise.

BARS
Eivissa
Bliss

Cocktail bar just outside Dalt Vila where Salvador Dalí's son concocts the *caparinhas* and *moquitos*.
Plaça des Parc 25. No tel.

Km 5

Km 5 takes its name from its location and is one of the most hip venues on the island. The resident DJs play cutting-edge funk, house and techno music. Dancing continues until late, licence permitting, and the vegetarian-friendly food is good, too.
Caretera Sant Josep 5.6km.
Tel: (971) 39 63 49. Open: daily June–Sept; Oct–May, Wed, Fri & Sat.

La Muralla

Friendly and extremely popular gay bar in the heart of Dalt Vila, with a small outdoor terrace.
Sa Carrossa 3, Dalt Vila, Eivissa.
Tel: (971) 30 18 83. Open: Easter–Nov.

Sa Botiga

Classy café-bar in the New Town, with rattan chairs, monochrome photographs on the walls and a delightful patio terrace to the rear. Good coffee, tapas and Guinness.
Avda Ignaci Wallis 14. No tel.

Sunset Café

Café bar on one of Eivissa's quieter squares, offering a relaxed ambience. Perfect for leafing through the newspaper over a leisurely continental breakfast. Small outdoor terrace.
Plaça des Parc 8. Tel: (971) 39 44 46.

Teatro Pereira
Though no longer a theatre, the first neocolonial-style building in Eivissa is still a major live music venue hosting regular jazz concerts. The café, in what was the foyer, stays open until 5am during the summer. Drinks are expensive, though.
Carrer Comte Rosselló 3, Eivissa. Tel: (971) 19 48 68.

Zurito
Currently one of the most fashionable bars in the port area with pre-clubbers. The reasonable drinks prices make it especially popular with young Spaniards.
Carrer Lluis Tur i Palau 3. No tel.

Platja d'en Bossa
Bora Bora
One of the island's best known beach bars, Bora Bora is the favourite of the clubbing fraternity who wander in here from nearby Space. The music (techno, house and trance) is in the hands of the resident DJs. Drinks prices are surprisingly reasonable and you can eat here, too. Closes around midnight.
Platja d'en Bossa. Tel: (971) 33 97 72.

Sant Antoni
Bar M
M for Manumission, the promoters who own the bar. Across the road from Es Paradis, this pre-clubbing venue is especially popular with the British. Music comes courtesy of the resident DJs. Food is strictly of the cheeseburger variety, although chicken in chilli sauce (*piri piri*) is the speciality of the new restaurant.
Avda. Dr Fleming s/n, Sant Antoni. No tel. Open: May–Oct.

Café del Mar
The original sunset bar, this was also the birthplace of the chillout compilation, though the original DJ, José Padilla, has moved on to Mambo. Arrive before 7pm to be sure of a seat; otherwise, sit out on the rocks and admire the view.
Sunset Strip (Carrer Vara del Rey), Sant Antoni. Tel: (971) 34 25 16. Open: Apr–Oct.

Café Mambo
DJs and promoters like to drop in here after Café del Mar has closed for the night. Famous for its pre-club parties featuring guest DJs.
Sunset Strip (Carrer Vara del Rey), Sant Antoni. Tel: (971) 34 66 38. Open: late May–Oct.

Coastline
A bar to beat all bars since it opened in 2001, Coastline also has a restaurant (expensive), a shop, three swimming pools, a sun terrace, music and much more besides.
Caló des Moro. Tel: (971) 34 85 53.

Kanya
Popular with sunset-watchers and house music enthusiasts, this bar-restaurant (Thai food) has a large pool and terrace. Dancing until 4am, licence permitting, but the drinks are expensive.
Caló des Moro. No tel.

Sant Carles
Anita's Bar
A hippie haunt back in the 1970s, Anita's is still going strong, thanks to its warm, friendly atmosphere and very good pub grub – tapas on the patio, full meals inside. It also serves the local liqueur *Hierbas Ibicencas*.
Sant Carles village (look for the sign near the bus stop). *No tel.*

Las Dalias

Best known for its Saturday hippie market, Las Dalias is a venue for special events, usually of the psychedelic variety, but occasionally also good rock and jazz concerts. Wednesday is *Nameste* night, when they serve up a three-course Indian meal to the sound of 'world music'. Tapas are served in the bar which stays open until 2.30am.
Ctra. Santa Eularia-Sant Carles 12km. Tel: (971) 19 22 43.

Sant Joan de Labritja

Eco Centre

'New-Age Bazaar', bar and Internet café with a pleasant garden round the back. Closes 9pm.
Plaça de Espanya, Sant Joan. No tel.

Santa Agnès

Can Cosmi

Typical village bar with a great atmosphere, a terrace overlooking the church and down-to-earth prices.
Santa Agnès. Tel: (971) 80 50 20. Closed Tue.

Santa Eulària

Guaramá

The only genuine nightclub in town, with guest DJs playing mainly funk-house and chillout. Some live performances.
Marina de Santa Eulària. No tel. Stays open until 6am.

Santa Gertrudis

Can Costa

Where the Spanish cured hams (*Jamon Serrano*) dangle from the roof before being sliced and served up in mouthwatering *bocadillos* (bread rolls), *tostadas* and *tortilla de la casa*. Some of the island's best contemporary artists showcase their work here.
Plaça de l'Església. Tel: (971) 19 70 21.

CLUBS

When going clubbing, most visitors pay at the door, although it is cheaper and more convenient to pick up an advance ticket (available from some bars). Prices are high (anything from 30–60 euros, depending on the season and what's on) and on top of that there are the drinks – a bottle of water will set you back another 6 euros. Some fliers offer a price reduction and/or a free drink and you can also save money by doing your drinking beforehand. Prices in the bars in Ibiza port and on Caló des Moro in Sant Antoni ('Sunset Strip'), are far from exorbitant and the atmosphere is more relaxed. People start arriving at around midnight and head off to the clubs around 1.30am. Generally speaking, there are no dress codes – only football shirts and beachwear are unacceptable. Sleeping on the beach is illegal and drink-driving laws are more rigorously enforced than on the mainland, with spot checks commonplace. While drugs like ecstasy are freely available, they are illegal and it will be up to the police to decide whether what you are carrying is for personal consumption or with the intention of dealing.

The clubs

The action centres around the 'big seven': Amnesia, Privilege, Pacha, El Divino, Space (an 'after hours' club open during the day), Es Paradis and Eden. First-time visitors will be impressed by the sheer scale of these mega-venues with their chillout zones and 'alternative rooms', split-level terraces and palm gardens, bars, restaurants and pools. The dance floor at Privilege can hold up to 10,000 spectators and is the size of a football pitch. What matters to discerning clubbers, however, is not the surroundings but the quality of entertainment offered by the promoters. Cream, Ministry of Sound, Manumission, Cocoon, GodsKitchen, each of these profit-driven outfits promises not only the best music but the ultimate party experience. Manumission set the pace back in 1994 with a show that combined elements of circus, carnival and theatre to calculatedly bizarre effect. Turn up to one of their parties at Privilege and you will still be entertained by transvestite trapeze artists, high-kicking showgirls, strippers and pole dancers, clowns and dwarves. Less provocative but no less popular are Amnesia's foam parties, while Eden's sunken dance floor is transformed into a huge swimming pool when it hosts a *fiesta del agua* (water party). Promoters always hold something in reserve for the opening and closing nights of the season when tickets are at a premium and queues are already forming early in the evening. When all is said and done, though, it is the music that matters.

Amnesia
Ctra Eivissa-Sant Antoni 5km. Tel: (971) 19 80 41. www.amnesia.es
Anfora
Ibiza's only gay club is in a natural cave and attracts an international mixed-age crowd. Resident DJs.
Carrer Sant Carles 7, Dalt Vila, Eivissa. Open: May–Oct.

Eden
Carrer Salvador Espriu, Sant Antoni. Tel: (971) 34 07 37. www.edenibiza.com
El Divino
Puerto Deportivo, Passeig Maritim, Eivissa. Tel: (971) 19 01 76. www.eldivino-ibiza.com
Es Paradis
Carrer Salvador Espriu, Sant Antoni. Tel: (971) 34 60 00. www.esparadis.com
Flower Power
Formentera's only genuine dance club is fairly low-key and plays house music and mainstream clubbing sounds. *Es Pujols, on Sant Ferran Road, Formentera. Open: June–Sept.*
Pacha
Avda 8 d'Agost, Passeig Maritim, Eivissa. Tel: (971) 31 36 12. www.pacha.es
Privilege
Ctra Eivissa-Sant Antoni 6km. Tel: (971) 19 81 60.
Space
Platja d'en Bossa. Tel: (971) 39 67 93. www.space-ibiza.com

CLUBBING

The choice of music depends on the club and the promoter, but in the course of a season you can hear everything under the sun. House, garage, techno and trance prevail, but the chillout zones offer funk, soul, R&B, salsa, gansta rap, hip hop – you name it. The clubs hire some of the world's most hip and respected DJs. Jazzy M, Judge Jules, Erick Morillo, Fat Boy Slim, Julian Amour and Sven Väth are household gods to the cognoscenti. They earn small fortunes and attract a loyal and devoted following.

Children

Ibiza is a child-friendly destination where the biggest attraction is the numerous beaches with gently shelving soft sand and shallow, clear water. Some of the best bucket-and-spade resorts are on the east coast: Cala Llonga and Es Canar can both be reached by boat from Santa Eulària and the ferry ride adds to the enjoyment.

Aguamar waterpark

Aquarium
Aquario Cap Blanc
Some boat excursions from Sant Antoni include a stop at this natural cave, now an aquarium. Half the pleasure for children lies in the illuminated grotto setting. Turtles, lobster, octopuses, rays, wrasse, moray eels and other Balearic marine species swim in the shallow waters of the cave floor, while the youngsters look down from a wooden walkway.
Ten minutes' walk from Cala des Moro (take the path from Hotel Tanit).
Open: Apr–Oct, 10am–sunset.

Bowling Centre
A large complex in the shopping area of Platja d'en Bossa. The facilities include a four-lane bowling alley with mini golf, pool tables and a safety-controlled mechanical bull thrown in.
Carrer Murtra 2–4, Platja d'en Bossa. Tel: (971) 30 03 56.

Can Marça Cave
(*See p79*)

Clothing
Laly's Nens
Boutique designed specifically with children in mind. Has a large and varied selection of designer clothes by Oilily, Versace and the like.
Joan d'Austria /corner of Carrer Madrid, New Town, Eivissa.

Go-karting
A fun activity for adults as well as children of all ages. There are two circuits in Ibiza, one in Sant Antoni, the other in Santa Eulària. Both have twin-engined adult karts, junior karts, electric baby karts and bikes. Santa Eulària has the more attractive setting.

Ibiza's caves were once used as smugglers' dens

The wonders of the deep in the Cap Blanc aquarium

Go-Kart Santa Eulària
Also table football and games machines.
Ctra de Santa Eulària des Riu 5.7km.
Tel: (971) 31 77 44. Open: daily Apr–Oct
10am–9pm. Nov–Mar weekends and
holidays from 11am.

Karting
Floodlit at night.
Ctra Sant Antoni km 14, Sant Antoni.
Tel: (971) 34 38 05.

Horse riding
There are horse-riding schools in Ibiza
and Formentera, offering tuition for
children and adults and excursions
through lovely rural settings.
Escuela de Equitación Can Mayans,
Santa Gertrudis/Sant Llorenç road.
Tel: (971) 18 73 88.

Playgrounds
Family entertainment centre behind
Cala de Bou beach, with bouncy castle,
trampolenes, mini go-karts, boats and a
playground. For the adults there's an
amusement complex with ten-pin
bowling, café and bars.
Cami des Moli, Bahia de Sant Antoni.

Scenic train
An open-top tourist train departs from
the bus stop by the 'Egg' in Sant Antoni
on a two-hour excursion into the scenic
countryside around Santa Agnès de la
Corona, where there is a stop for a
drink. The train then continues to a
nearby *mirador* for great views.
There is a similar trip from Santa
Eulària (*see p60*).

Waterparks
Aguamar
The island's largest water park is just
100m (328ft) from the beach at Platja
d'en Bossa. Apart from some spectacular
rides, there is also a special picnic area,
shop and café. *Platja d'en Bossa.*
Tel: (971) 39 67 90. Open: daily May–Oct
10am–6pm.

Aqualandia
Marvel at the views of Eivissa bay while
the children hurtle down the
waterslides, toboggans, spirals and speed
chutes. Other amenities include
swimming pools with sunbeds, tennis
and squash courts and refreshment
points.
Cap Martinet-Platja Talamanca.
Tel: (971) 19 24 11. Open: daily
June–Sept 10am–6pm.

Sports and Leisure

Ibiza offers a wide variety of outdoor and leisure activities, from hiking and horse riding to canoeing and ballooning. Water-sports enthusiasts are particularly well catered for, with schools on most of the main beaches offering tuition and equipment hire. If the listings below do not include your favourite sport, consult the tourist offices in Eivissa and La Savina (Formentera).

Easy Rider Stables at Cala Llonga

Balloon flights
Minimum of two, maximum of six people, approximately 40-min flight. Allow four hours for transportation from hotel, tuition and snack.
Tel: (630) 410167.
www.ibizaenglobo.com/balloon

Boat charter and fishing trips
Barca Yaya II
Boat and fishing trips.
La Savina, Formentera. Tel: (609) 847 186.
Pesca Ibiza
Deep-sea fishing trips offered on a half-day basis.
Edificio Bristol, Avda 8 d'Agost, Eivissa.
Tel: (971) 31 44 91.
Santa Eulàlia Yachting S L
Day trips to Formentera and cruises to some of the lesser-known Ibizan coves.
Marina de Santa Eulària.
Tel: (971) 33 83 94.
Tagomago Charters
Boats and skippers for hire.
Port Esportiu Santa Eulària.
Tel: (971) 33 81 01.

Diving schools
Most schools offer introductory PADI-approved courses and a varied programme of dives. All equipment is included in the price.
Eivissa Best Dive
Carrer Cantabria, Sant Antoni.
Tel: (971) 80 41 25.
Punta Dive
Cala Martina (Punta Arabí).
Tel: (971) 33 67 26.
Vellmari Diving Centre
Marina Botafoc, Eivissa.
Tel: (971) 19 28 84.
Also at *Sa Savina, Formentera.*
Tel: (971) 32 21 05.
www.vellmari.com

Golf
For more information about golf on the island contact the Balearic Island Golf Federation.
Tel: (971) 72 27 53.
www.fbgolf.com

Hiking
EcoIbiza
Organises treks to some of the more out-of-the-way spots on the island. Half day or full day.
Carrer Abad y Lasierra 35, Eivissa.
Tel: (971) 30 23 47.
www.ecoibiza.com

Horse riding

Scenic excursions following coastal paths or into the woodland and hills of Ibiza and across the salt flats in Formentera.

Cuadra Es Puig
Can Puig estate, Santa Gertrudis.
Tel: (971) 19 71 66 or (607) 14 40 29.

Easy Rider
Camino Camping, Cala Llonga.
Tel: (971) 19 65 11.

Sahona Horses
Sant Francesc on Cap de Barbària road, Formentera. Tel: (971) 323 001.

Tennis

Club de Campo

Six clay tennis courts, two 'quick' surfaces and one squash court, all of which are floodlit. There's also a gym, sauna, swimming and tennis classes, and a snack bar.
Ctra Sant Josep 4km. Tel: (971) 30 00 88.

Water sports

Cesar's Watersports Rentals

Hires out jet skis and organises para-sailing, banana rides, water-skiing, and also boat hire.
Platja de S'Argamassa.

Club Delfin Vela y Windsurf

Offers tuition and board rental.
Hotel Delfin, Cala Codolar.
Tel: (971) 80 62 10.

Formentera Diving and Watersports

The best place to head for on the island for diving tuition, kayak and jet-ski rental, and boat hire.
Marina de La Savina, Formentera.
Tel: (971) 32 32 32.

Vela Náutica

This sailing school also rents out windsurfing equipment and kayaks.
Avda Dr Fleming, Sant Antoni.
Tel: (971) 34 65 35.

There are **water-skiing** schools on more than a dozen beaches across the island, including: Platja d'en Bossa, Ses Salines, Cala d'Hort, Caló des Moro, Port de Sant Miquel, Cala Llonga and Es Canar. There are **jet-ski** schools on the following beaches: Es Figueral, d'en Bossa, S'Argamassa, Sant Vicent and the river beach in Santa Eulària.

Yoga

Ibiza is becoming known as the yoga capital of Europe.

Ibiza Yoga

Specialises in Ashtanga, more aerobic-centred than traditional yoga. Instructors include Danny Paradise, who taught Sting, Kate Moss and Sadie Frost.
Cala Benirràs.
Tel: (UK 0044) 0207 419 0999.
www.ibizayoga.com. Open: May–Oct.

LA RUTA DE SAL

This famous yachting event began in 1846 when merchant seamen transporting salt from Ibiza to the mainland held a race to see which ship could make the crossing in the fastest time. The first modern race was held in 1989 and has been an annual event ever since, with more than 2,000 competitors and 300 vessels taking part. Before the regatta, which takes place in April, boats are divided into categories – classic, vintage, multihull, etc. Some set off from Barcelona, others from Denia, but all end up crossing the finishing line in Eivissa harbour.

Food and Drink

While Ibiza is not known for its gastronomy, it is possible to eat well on the island. The more sophisticated restaurants offer the best of Basque, Provençal and Catalan cuisine, while the more homely establishments specialise in rich and nourishing local dishes.

Waiter at Croissant Show, Ibiza Town

What to eat

Ibizan cooking is closely related to that of the other Balearic Islands where traditionally the inhabitants had to make do with simple, often scarce ingredients. Soups and stews are the mainstays, drawing on the produce of the land and sea and generously seasoned with herbs and spices.

Where and when to eat

While in Ibiza it makes sense to adapt to local customs of eating and drinking. Spaniards start the day with a light continental breakfast, usually a croissant or slice of toast washed down with a coffee or glass of fresh orange juice. Later in the morning, they will take another short break for a sandwich and possibly a glass of wine or beer. The main meal of the day is lunch (*la comida*), eaten at around 2pm, more often than not in a café or restaurant. Virtually every establishment offers a *menú del día*, a fixed-price, three-course meal including a drink. Typically, the choice of first courses will include a salad, a soup or two and possibly a paella; the second is a small selection of meat and fish dishes, followed by dessert – usually *flan* (crème caramel), rice pudding, fresh fruit or ice cream. If this sounds a bit much, look out for the list of *combinados*, one-course dishes which often include a drink or a side salad in the price. Lunch is sometimes followed at around 5 or 6pm by the *merienda*, another coffee, maybe with a cake or pastry (most Spaniards have a sweet tooth). Dinner (*cena*) is comparatively light and will not be eaten until around 10pm. A group of friends will often dispense with a formal meal in favour of sharing *tapas* – small plates of appetisers served at the counter in bars. The custom is to visit several bars, sampling a tapa or two in each. After a night at a club, Spaniards like to finish off with an early breakfast of *chocolate con churros*, a cup of thick hot chocolate served with long thin doughnuts for dipping into the drink. When dining out, it is always a good idea to book a table, at least in the more popular restaurants. The same goes for lunch on Sundays and public holidays when Spaniards eat out *en famille*. Kitchens close around 11pm in Ibiza but considerably earlier in Formentera (as a rule, bars also shut much earlier here, at least in the villages). VAT (IVA in Spanish) of 7 per cent is added to restaurant bills, but not a service charge. A tip of 5 per cent will suffice; 10 per cent will be seen as generous.

Some of the best Ibizan restaurants are

to be found away from the towns, along country roads or in other picturesque locations. Bear in mind, however, that the quality of the food in that charming farmhouse or harbour-front terrace will not *necessarily* live up to the setting. When choosing a restaurant, look for somewhere where the majority of customers are speaking one of the local languages. Steer clear of chains and places with picture menus or national flags. Eating out in Ibiza should be an informal and relaxed affair. Dress codes are rare and should be treated with suspicion.

Vegetarians

While Spain in general has been slow in acknowledging, let alone catering for, the needs of vegetarians, Ibiza is somewhat ahead of the game in this respect, although restaurants catering specifically for vegetarians and vegans are still thin on the ground. That said, in international restaurants at least, it should always be possible to find at least one vegetarian main course on the menu, while gourmet establishments will, if forewarned, prepare vegetarian or even vegan meals. It may be a different story, though, in the humble country inn or farmhouse, which may not be able to provide anything more exciting than soup, tomato salad or the dreaded omelette. It's best to double-check vegetarian-sounding dishes, as they are sometimes flavoured with ham or cod, or with animal stock.

Typical Ibizan meals and ingredients
Starters

Arròs sec – thick soup with rice, fish, shellfish and prawns, lightly fried chicken, rabbit and vegetables.

Cassoleta de patates – casserole made from potatoes, onion, tomato, garlic and parsley.
Olla fresca – casserole made from haricot beans, broad beans, potatoes and pears.
Pa torrat amb tomata – toasted bread, rubbed with tomato, with a dribble of olive oil and a sprinkling of salt (also eaten at breakfast).
Sopa de menuts – chicken giblet soup.
Sopa de pa – bread soup, enriched with beaten egg.
Truita pagesa – potato omelette made with peppers and tomatoes.

Meat dishes

Caragols – snails, cooked with cold meats and pork fat.
Conill amb pebrots vermells – rabbit with red peppers.
Costelletes de moltó – rib of lamb, particularly tasty when served with *prebassos*, a local wild mushroom.
Llom de porc – charcoal grilled loin of pork, seasoned with rosemary.
Perdiu amb col – partridge served with cabbage and potatoes.
Sobrassada i botifarrons – spicy sausage meat, served with pork fat, potatoes and chicken broth.
Sofrit pagès – rich, hold-all hotpot, including Balearic sausage, pork, potatoes, onions, tomatoes, fried peppers and herbs.

Fish dishes

Amanida de peix – fish salad, a speciality of Formentera.
Bullit de peix – fish stew with potatoes, vegetables and chick peas.
Burrida de ratjada – stew made with

potatoes and ray fish, cooked in a wine and spice stock with pulverised almonds and sometimes a few drops of pastis liqueur added.

Caldereta de langusta – substantial lobster stew, originating in Menorca, cooked in a wooden casserole dish with onion, tomato, garlic and parsley.

Guisat de peix – fish stew made with grouper, bream, angler, scorpion fish or any other fresh fish available, plus garlic, onion, saffron, parsley, potatoes and cinnamon.

Tonyina a l'evissenca – tuna seasoned with white wine, raisins, eggs, pine kernels, spices and lemon.

Desserts

Bunyols – small potato doughnuts, sprinkled with sugar.

Flaó – tart made with eggs, cheese, flour, sugar, aniseed and mint. Traditionally eaten at Easter.

Greixonera – the local version of crème caramel, made with egg yolks, milk and sugar, broken biscuits, with cinnamon and a slice of lemon. Sometimes with a few drops of *frígola* liqueur added.

Orelletes – popular cakes made with sugar and dried fruits.

Drinks

Frígola – Ibizan liqueur extracted from thyme with an anise base.

Hierbas Ibicencas – popular liqueur flavoured with many herbs, including aniseed, thyme and rosemary, serve chilled with a twist of lemon and orange peel.

Palo – Ibizan aperetif to be taken with a few drops of gin.

Vi de taula pages – table wine. The quality of Ibizan table wines (whites and reds) has improved noticeably in recent years (*see p170*). The same cannot be said for the rougher Formenteran varieties.

Spanish tapas

Aceitunas – green or black olives, sometimes stuffed with pepper or baby gherkins.

Anchoas – anchovies, usually served in vinegar. (Also known as *boquerrones*.)

Berberechos – cockles.

Chorizo – spicy sausage, served in the same way as *Jamón Serrano*.

Croquetas – made with thick, béchamel sauce, chicken or chopped ham, and then deep-fried.

Ensaladilla russa – Russian salad, with potatoes, vegetables and mayonnaise.

Gambas – shrimps grilled in their shells (*a la plancha*) or peeled and then fried in oil and garlic (*al ajillo*).

Jamón Serrano – cured ham, served on its own, in slices.

Morcilla – very rich black pudding.

Patatas alioli – boiled potatoes with garlic and mayonnaise dressing.

Pimientos rellenos – peppers stuffed with meat, tuna or cod.

Pulpo – octopus.

Queso manchego – cheese made from sheep's milk, often coated with olive oil.

RESTAURANTS
Meal prices

Prices at Ibizan restaurants can vary widely in price. Prices in this guide are subject to fluctuation and should only be used as a rough guide.

*	Under €60	**	€60–€80
***	€80–€100	****	Over €100

Balàfia
Balàfia*
Grilled meat dishes, cooked to perfection over a wood fire, are the speciality of this charming restaurant opposite Ca na Pepeta (*see below*).
Sant Llorenç, Ctra. de Sant Joan 15.4 km. Tel: (971) 32 50 19. Open: May–Dec evenings only.
Ca na Pepeta**
Off a little side turning towards Santa Eulària, this restored farmhouse serves delicious regional cooking at affordable prices. Book ahead if possible.
Sant Llorenç, Ctra. de Sant Joan 15.4 km. Tel: (971) 33 33 77.

Cala Boix
La Noria**
There are lovely sea views from this unassuming restaurant overlooking the beach, where the house speciality is the Balearic lobster stew, c*aldereta de langosta.*
Cala Boix. Tel: (971) 63 88 06 /33 53 97.

Cala Carbó
Restaurante Balneario**
José Prats has been delighting the customers of his Carbó beach seafood restaurant for more than a quarter of a century. The perfect surroundings for a *guisado de pescado* or *arroz a la banda.*
Tel: (971) 34 17 66. Open: until end Oct.

Cala Gracioneta
El Chiringuito**
Not just any *chiringuito*. Here the barbecued meat and swordfish steaks are served almost at the water's edge, and the lighting is provided by candles floating on the water. *Tel: (971) 34 83 38. Open: May–Oct.*

Cala d'Hort
Es Boldado*
Friendly *chiringuito* restaurant only a 5-minute walk from the beach. The seafood menu includes lobster and a small choice of typical Ibizan dishes, but the big draw is the view of Es Vedrà. Booking advisable.
Cala d'Hort. Tel: (626) 49 45 37.

Cala Jondal
Bar Particular**
Well-known beach bar where the beautiful people chill. Mainly barbecued meats and fish salads, is on the pricey side, but the clientele is more interested in the performance of the DJs.
No tel. Open: May–Oct.

Tropicana***
Thatched roof, flower-bedded patio and sea views are the trademarks of this bar-restaurant on the right of the beach as you leave the car park. The fish casseroles are a safe bet, and Sunday is Brazilian night, with a live samba band.
Cala Jondal. Tel: (971) 18 75 20. Open: May–Sept.

Cala Mastella
El Bigote**
Balmy location in a tiny inlet hidden by rocks. The boss, nicknamed 'The Moustache' (El Bigote), catches the fish himself before cooking them. One of the best places on the island to try the Ibizan speciality, *bullit de peix/guixat de peix.* Tables are at a premium and you need to reserve in person – they do not take phone bookings – several days in advance. A lot of trouble but worth the effort.
Carrer Jaume Torres. Tel: (971) 63 37 15.

Cala Salada
Cala Salada*
Ibizan cooking at its no-frills best, right on the doorstep of one of the island's most arresting beaches. The fish comes straight from the owners' boat.
Platja de Cala Salada. Tel: (971) 34 28 67.

Cala Sant Vicent
Can Gat**
Authentic Ibizan seafood restaurant with terrace overlooking the beach. *Caldereta de langosta* to die for.
Cala Sant Vicent. Tel: (971) 32 01 23/ 82 01 28. Open: Apr–Nov.

Cala Vedella
Maria Luisa***
Family-run establishment at the far end of the beach, serving typical fish and seafood dishes, including mouthwatering crab. Booking advised at weekends.
Cala Vedella. Tel: (971) 80 80 12. Open: daily.

Eivissa
Can Alfredo**
One of Eivissa's best-known restaurants. Offers a large selection of typical Ibizan dishes, including a hearty *sofrit pagès* and an equally delicious *arroz con sepia* (cuttlefish served with rice). Meticulous service and attention to detail.
Passeig de Vara de Rey 16. Tel: (971) 31 12 74. Closed Mon.

Can den Parra***
Dine by candlelight on the steps of a vine-covered terrace in Dalt Vila. Flavoursome, Spanish Mediterranean cooking – try the sautéed goats' cheese to start with, then the grilled sea bass made from an old Spanish recipe. Booking recommended throughout August.
Calle San Rafael 3. Tel: (971) 39 11 14/ 30 39 01. Open: May–Oct, evenings only.

El Bistro**
Subtly prepared French Mediterranean cooking is the hallmark of this restaurant in the heart of Dalt Vila. The menu changes regularly, but if they have the duck magret in fig sauce, look no further. Should you be unable to find a table in the dining room, there is an outdoor terrace.
Sa Carrossa 15. Tel: (971) 39 32 03. Open: Apr–Oct.

El Cigarral***
This restaurant in a prettily decorated house in the port area has a reputation for sophisticated Mediterranean cooking. Castilian-Spanish influences are at work in the more creative dishes.
Fray Vincente Nicolas 9. Tel: (971) 31 12 46. Open: daily except Sun evening.

El Olivo***
This classy French restaurant in Dalt Vila is renowned throughout the island for its refined Provençal cuisine, extensive wine list, refined ambience and attentive service. Booking essential.
Carrer de Santa Creu 2. Tel: (971) 30 06 80. Open: evenings only.

Formentera**
The place to sample the best of traditional Ibizan cooking. Outstanding fish and rice dishes, and the desserts are good too.
Carrer Lluís Tur i Palau. Tel: (971) 31 10 24. Open: daily.

Hong Kong★★
It may be short on atmosphere, but the Shanghai and Cantonese cooking in this typical Chinese restaurant, a few minutes' walk from Vara del Rey, is up to scratch. Good-value *menú del día* and takeaway service.
Calle Vincente Cuervo 13.
Tel: (971) 31 17 56.

La Brasa★★★
Always in vogue thanks to its lovely, bougainvillea-scented garden in summer and log fire in winter. The extensive menu of grilled meat and fish dishes varies according to the season. Booking recommended.
Calle Pere Sala 3. Tel: (971) 30 12 02.
Open: lunch and dinner. Closed Sun & Feb.

Mesón de Paco★
Traditional Ibizan recipes (rice-based dishes a speciality), down-to-earth prices and an attractive, rustic-style décor have made this restaurant in the new town an established hit with foreign visitors.
Avda. de Bartomeu de Rosselló 15.
Tel: (971) 31 42 24.

Restaurant Victoria★
Traditional Spanish *comedor* with plain furnishings and friendly staff. Good selection of reasonably-priced Spanish and Ibizan meat and fish dishes. Expect to queue in high season and note that the kitchen closes early (around 11pm).
Calle Riambau 1, La Marina.
Tel: (971) 31 06 22.

Sa Torreta★★★
As the name suggests, this chic French restaurant on Dalt Vila's main square is located in one of Calvi's Renaissance bastions (if you can't get a table inside there's usually room on the terrace).
Plaça de la Vila. Tel: (971) 30 04 11.
Open: May–Oct.

Figueretes
De Gouwe Haan★★
Incredibly popular, this large restaurant is on one of the streets immediately behind the beach. The huge menu is international, but the tastiest dishes come from the former Dutch colony of Suriname.
Carrer Galicias s/n. No tel.

Soleado★★★
There are at least two reasons for recommending this French restaurant. One is the views of Formentera from the terrace, the other, wonderfully delicate Provençal cooking prepared by the Avignon-trained chef.
Paseo ses Pitiusas s/n.
Tel: (971) 39 48 11. Open: May–Oct.

Sant Agusti
Can Berri Vell★★
Wonderfully atmospheric farmhouse in a village in the heart of the Ibizan countryside. The aroma of grilled meat emanating from the terrace has lured many a casual visitor.
Plaça Major. Tel: (971) 34 43 21. Open: Sept–June Thur–Sat; July–Aug daily.

Sant Antoni de Portmany
Can Pujol★
Small beach restaurant with a seaside terrace, tucked between the bars and hotels of Port des Torrent. The pick of the fish and seafood dishes is the house

speciality, *guisat de piex.*
Port des Torrent. Tel: (971) 34 14 07.
Open: daily except Wed & Dec.

Es Pi d'Or**

Located at the northern end of the Bahía de Sant Antoni, this restaurant serves fish and seafood dishes based on Galician (northern Spanish) recipes. The judiciously chosen wine list is an additional recommendation.
Urbanización Cap Negret.
Tel: (971) 34 28 72.
Open: daily except Dec–Feb.

Sa Capella***

This restaurant on the road towards Santa Agnès has acquired a certain cachet thanks to the rich and famous among its clientele. The jury is out on the quality of the food, but no one will argue that the location, an abandoned 18th-century church, is anything but evocative.
Cami de Cas Ramons, off Ctra. Sant Antoni-Santa Agnès. Tel: (971) 34 00 57.
Open: Apr–Oct evenings.

Sant Josep
Can Bernat Vinye*

Village life centres on this humble bar where you can sample excellent Spanish tapas and local Ibizan wines. The terrace overlooks the main square.
Plaça de l'Església.

El Destino*

Friendly bar-restaurant in the centre of the village with a great line in Spanish tapas, with a hint of fusion. There's plenty of choice, and vegetarians will not be disappointed. Couscous and tagine dishes on Moroccan nights (Friday).

Booking essential on the terrace.
Carrer Atalaya 15. Tel: (971) 80 03 41.
Open: daily except Sun.

Sant Rafael
Ayoun***

For an echo of Ibiza's Arab past, try this superb Moroccan restaurant just north of the village. Both the interior décor and Bedouin tented garden are Moorish-inspired. Expensive but worth it.
Ctra Eivissa-Sant Antoni.
Tel: (971) 19 85 45.
Open: daily Easter–Oct.

El Clos Denis***

Renowned for its superb Provençal cooking, this restaurant is located in an old house opposite the church. Book ahead for a table on the terrace.
Plaça de l'Església. Tel: (971) 19 85 45.
Open: daily Apr–Oct.

Santa Eulària des Riu
Bambuddha Grove***

Currently one of the trendiest hang-outs in Ibiza, Bambuddha Grove serves an eclectic mix of fusion dishes, prepared by executive chef Grégor Marx, and best described as Asian-Mediterranean. Guests dine by candlelight beneath a pyramid roof made from reeds and bamboo.
Ctra. de Sant Joan 8.5km.
Tel: (971) 19 75 10.
www.bambuddha.com
Open: May–Oct daily, evenings only; Nov–Apr Thur–Sun evenings only.

Ca Na Ribes***

Restaurant with a distinguished pedigree for serving Ibizan and Mediterranean fish

and meat dishes to a loyal, appreciative clientele. Lovely indoor patio.
Sant Vincent 44. Tel: (971) 33 00 06.
Open: Apr–Oct daily except Tue.

Celler C'an Pere***
Wine casks and wood-beamed ceilings are the main decorative features of this large restaurant. The fresh fish is cooked to perfection and worth splashing out for.
Carrer de Sant Jaume 63.
Tel: (971) 33 08 84.
Open: daily, evenings only.

The Royalty**/***
One of the oldest café-restaurants on the island, the Royalty was a Fascist haunt during the Civil War, according to American writer, Elliot Paul. The café serves up good breakfasts and desserts, while at the back you'll find an exclusive restaurant with an international *à la carte* menu.
Sant Jaume 51. Tel: (971) 33 18 19.

FORMENTERA
Caló de Sant Agustí
Rafalet**
This large waterfront restaurant prides itself on its Balearic fish and seafood dishes. The *bullit de peix* should not be overlooked. Reservations essential.
Caló de Sant Agusti.
Tel: (971) 32 70 77.
Open: May–Sept.

El Pilar de La Mola
El Mirador**
Located fairly discreetly at the right-hand side of the road, so the breathtaking views of Formentera (you really can

see the entire island from the terrace) come as something of a surprise. The food – paella, grilled fish and a selection of rice dishes – can't quite compete. Booking essential in July and August.
Ctra de La Mola 14km.
Tel: (971) 32 70 37. Open: May–Oct.

La Pequeña Isla*
This unassuming roadside restaurant (with terrace) serves up simple island fare: roast rabbit, lamb and rice-based dishes.
Ctra de la Mola, El Pilar.
Tel: (971) 32 70 68.

Es Pujols
Ca Minito/***
This Argentinian steakhouse has been around for more than 20 years and is the real McCoy, with a melt-in-the-mouth *asado de tira bife*. Prices are according to weight.
Ctra. Es Pujols-La Savina.
Tel: (971) 32 81 06.
www.rte-caminito.com
Open: Apr–Nov, evenings only.

Sa Savina
Aigüa**
Restaurant with a touch of class and a terrace looking out onto the marina. Spanish and international dishes.
La Savina harbour. Tel: (971) 32 33 22.
Open: May–Sept.

Sant Ferran
Las Ranas*
Classy French cuisine, certainly the best to be found on Formentera. Expect to pay for the privilege.
Carrer Embaxeter. Tel: (971) 32 81 95.

Ibizan Wines

A small bodega near Sant Josep recently caused a minor sensation when one of its wines was chosen for special mention at a tasting organised by an influential trade magazine. Praise indeed for a region that was not even on the viniculture map until the 1990s. The wine in question, Es Diví sa selecció 2001, was produced by Vins de Tanys Mediterranis, one of four bodegas on the island.

Modest beginnings

Wine was introduced to Ibiza by the Phoenicians in the 6th or 7th century BC – amphorae from the Pitiusas have been found in a number of ports around the Mediterranean, especially off the Valencian coast of Spain. Techniques improved during the Roman occupation when, it is said, orgiastic rites were celebrated with the encouragement of Bacchus himself. Following the expulsion

of the Moors in the 13th century, Jaume I was quick to grant new licences to aspiring winegrowers, but there were few takers in Ibiza. When Archduke Ludwig Salvator of Austria visited the island in 1867, he reported seeing only a tiny amount of land under cultivation, and this was before the phylloxera blight arrived from France. The wine that did eventually reach the table was coarse, and all of it was consumed before the following harvest. It was not until the 1980s that a handful of enterprising producers decided to invest in modern technology in a move to improve the quality of local wine. The gambit paid off: in 1996 the Balearic government was sufficiently impressed to designate Ibiza and Formentera a region with wines of a distinctive character – *Vinos de la Tierra* in the official parlance. The aim now is to go one better and gain Ibizan Regional Wines the coveted *Denominacion de Origen* (DO) status.

A growing business

The land under cultivation, currently around 130 hectares (0.5 sq mile), yields a modest 420hl (55 cubic yds) per annum but there are plans to expand if all goes well. Fifty per cent of the wine comes from the San Mateu valley and most of that from Joan Bonet's bodega at Sa Cova. There are three other wineries on the island: Vins de Tanys (*see above*), Can Maymó and Can Rich de Buscastell near Sant Antoni.

Conditions for growing wine are good – the reddish soil is rich in limestone and the climate typically Mediterranean with plenty of sunshine, mild winters and a modest amount of rainfall.

Traditionally, producers favoured the red Monastrell and Garnacha grapes and the Malabeo for the whites, but the new vineyards are experimenting with Cabernet Sauvignon, Merlot and Syrah (red) and Chardonnay, Muscatel or Viognier (white). One of the more unusual characteristics of Ibizan wine is the hint of aromatic herbs – thyme is used to prevent the blocking of the vats during fermentation. To date, varieties are almost exclusively *vinos de crianza* (table wines), but the quality is improving all the time. Who knows, Ibizan wines may, at the very least, be able to give the vineyards of Mallorca a run for their money.

Where to taste

The yield from the new harvest is showcased in December at the San Mateu wine festival. Otherwise, informal tours can be arranged in advance with either Sa Cova (*tel: (971) 187 046*) or Can Rich (*tel: (971) 805 100*). Local wines are on sale at Es Trui de Can Andreu and at restaurants specialising in Ibizan cuisine.

Opposite: The Ibizan liqueur *Hierbas Ibicencas* works well as an aperitif

Hotels and Accommodation

Between them, Ibiza and Formentera receive more than 1,850,000 visitors every year, and the number of hotel beds is continually increasing to meet the demand. Bear in mind, however, that package tour companies block-book much of the medium-priced accommodation during July and August when finding a room of any kind can be difficult.

Terrace views are a feature of many hotels on the islands

While there is only one five-star hotel in the Pitiusas (Hotel Hacienda in Na Xamena), visitors can choose from the full range of accommodation, from luxury hotels with every conceivable amenity to the humble pension or hostel. Apartments outnumber hotels on Formentera, and at the height of the season demand outstrips supply. Generally speaking, prices are somewhat higher than on the mainland, but outside the peak season most establishments offer big reductions, so it is worth shopping around.

The Associació d'Agroturisme Balear is an organisation offering alternative holidays in idyllic, natural surroundings far from the madding crowd. There are currently around a dozen hotels of this type on Ibiza (none on Formentera), mostly converted farmhouses in extensive grounds. Facilities tend to be luxurious and are priced accordingly. Horse riding and other country pursuits (special hiking tours, for example) are often available.

Below is a selection of hotels and other accommodation on both islands. Unless otherwise indicated, they can be assumed to have ensuite facilities, telephone and TV. Most hotels accept payment by credit card, but some of the cheaper pensions insist on cash.

Booking

Booking ahead is always advisable and an absolute must if you plan to visit during *Semana Santa* (Holy Week), during the local ferias (*see list on p22*) or in the high season (roughly from the middle of July to the end of August). Hotels will hold rooms until 6pm, or later if you warn them of your estimated arrival time, but some may require pre-booking by credit card. Be warned that many do not quote prices inclusive of 17 per cent IVA, Spain's value-added tax. Checkout is usually at noon, but most hotels will keep bags or even let you use the room until later if asked.

Prices

The prices shown according to the star system are average summertime prices for a double room. Suites and rooms during premium periods will be extra.

*	under €60	**	€60–120
***	€120–180	****	€180–300

Bahía de Sant Antoni
Aparthotel Nereida ***
Conveniently situated between the town
(4km (2.5 miles)) and Port des Torrent
beach, most of these comfortable
apartments in an attractive garden
setting have sea views, restaurant, pool
and night-time entertainment.
Port des Torrent. Tel: (971) 34 33 62.
Blau Parc*
This small attractively priced hotel, near
'happening' Caló d'es Moro beach, has
simply furnished but comfortable
rooms, all with air conditioning, satellite
TV and terrace. Large pool and café-
snack bar, but no restaurant. Studio
apartments also available.
Calle Velázquez 9, Sant Antoni de
Portmany. Tel: (971) 34 81 31.
www.grupolasirena.com
Fiesta Aptos. Cap Nono**
Appealing, fully-equipped studios and
apartments (the latter with terraces) at
the northern end of the bay. Peace and
quiet in an attractive garden setting,
close to the sea, or there's a swimming
pool if you prefer.
Cap Nono s/n. Tel: (971) 34 07 50.
www.fiesta-hotels.com
Fiesta Hotel San Diego*
Friendly, completely refurbished hotel
on the cliffs overlooking Port des
Torrent beach and only 5km (3 miles)
from town. Facilities include swimming
pools, tennis courts and air-conditioned
restaurant. All in all, good value.
Port d'es Torrent. Tel: (971) 34 08 50.
www.fiesta-hotels.com
Hostal Residencia Salada*
An excellent budget option, the rooms
in this small, centrally located hotel are
spotless and a good size. Only some

have balconies and ensuite bathrooms,
though, so book well ahead.
Calle Soletat 24. Tel: (971) 34 11 30.
Open: Easter–Oct.
Hotel-Club Els Pins**
Large, modern hotel with pool, set in
attractive pine-wooded parkland
between Cala Pinyet and S'Estanyol.
The rooms (some recently renovated)
are simply furnished but airy. Facilities
include bike hire, tennis and volleyball
courts, a sailing school and a diving
school.
Carrer des Calo, 07820.
Tel: (971) 34 03 01.
www.ibiza-hotels.com/elspins-en
Osiris Ibiza*
All 97 rooms in this family-run hotel
overlooking the beach at Es Puet (50m
(164ft)) are spacious and airy and have
sea or garden views. Buffet-restaurant
and swimming pool. Excellent value.
Platja Es Puet. Tel: (971) 34 09 16.
www.hotelosiris.com
Pike's **
Situated in the heart of the countryside,
yet less than 5 minutes' drive from the
sea. The rambling 15th-century
farmhouse and grounds have been
transformed into a stylish hotel with 40
handsome bedrooms and suites. Excellent
restaurant, floodlit swimming pool and
tennis court, gym and sauna.
Cami de Sa Vorera 12 km.
Tel: (971) 34 22 22.
www.ibiza-hotels.com/pikes
Vistabella*
'Beautiful view' just about sums up this
complex of 11 luxury bungalows in lovely
grounds about 25 minutes' walk from
town and with a stunning bay outlook.
All rooms have tasteful furnishings and a

terrace. Large pool and riding school nearby for those into country pursuits.
Camí de Benamussi 07820.
Tel: (971) 34 23 24.

Cala Boix
Hostal Cala Boix*
Location, location, location – in this case, pine woods with an outlook over the stunning beach at Cala Boix. Simply furnished, attractive rooms with sea or mountain views and breakfast thrown in. Great value.
Calle Cala Boix Sant Carles.
Tel: (971) 33 52 24.

Cala Molí
Hostal Cala Molí**
Family hostel in a wooded setting with easy access to some of the island's best coves and beaches. The eight double rooms, tastefully decorated in rustic style, are built around a small pool and terrace overlooking the sea.
1km (0.6 mile) south of Cala Moli.
Tel: (971) 80 60 02.
www.calamoli.com

Cala Tarida
Club Green Oasis Cala Tarida**
Large resort hotel with an attractive garden setting, near one of Ibiza's most celebrated beaches. Rooms have been recently refurbished and facilities are top-notch: two swimming pools (one for children), children's playground, tennis and squash courts, clubhouse with bar and restaurant. An excellent family option.
Plaza del Mar,
Tel: (971) 80 62 68.
www.ibiza-hotels.com/cala-tarida

Cala Vedella
Caló d'en Real
Golf fans take note: this classy hotel with its own private bay, accessed on foot, offers special fees for the Roca Llisa golf course as part of the deal, and has its own driving range and putting green (tuition available). Other attractions include a quality restaurant serving international cuisine, tennis courts and panoramic sea views from the pool.
Urbanización Calo d'en Real, San Josep de Sa Talaia, 07830. Tel: (971) 80 80 01.
www.hotelvillage.net
Club Aquarium**
Situated in an attractive garden about 400m (0.25 mile) from the bay and one of Ibiza's most pleasant resorts, each of these 115 well-spaced apartments comes fully equipped for self-catering, with half-board also available. Facilities include a children's pool and playground, tennis courts, restaurant and supermarket. Well suited to families.
Tel: (971) 80 81 00.

EIVISSA
El Corsario*
This one-time pirates' den in the heart of Dalt Vila was the home of the famous 19th-century corsair, Antoni Riquer. The 14 smallish rooms have beamed roofs and antique furnishings (ask for one with a harbour view). Attractive rates out of season.
Poniente 5, 07800. Tel: (971) 39 32 12.
El Palacio***
A more upmarket alternative to El Corsario, also within the walls of Dalt Vila. The décor in each room is inspired by a movie star of yesteryear and is unashamedly kitsch. Rooms have all mod

cons, but not all have their own terrace.
Calle de la Conquista 2, 07800.
Tel: (971) 30 14 78. www.elpalacio.com
Hostal Mar Blau**
Wonderful sea views from this small,
family hotel on Puig des Molins, only a
short walk from the centre of town.
Rooms, though strictly no-frills, are
attractive enough and each has its own
balcony or terrace. Soak up the sun on
the roof-top solarium. Bar and dining
room but no restaurant.
Calle Los Molinos, Puig des Molins.
Tel: (971) 30 12 84. Open: May–Oct.
Hostal Parque **
Definitely the best budget option in
town, this medium-sized *hostal* (29
rooms) is only a stone's throw from the
walls of Dalt Vila. Though on the small
side, rooms are pristine and nicely
turned out, with air conditioning and
TV. Not all have baths. The roof-top sun
terrace is a definite plus. Popular, so
advance booking is essential.
Plaça des Parc 4. Tel: (971) 30 13 58.
Royal Plaza****
Modern hotel with comfortable
rooms and all mod cons. The main
recommendation, though, apart from
the Le Relais restaurant, has to be the
roof-top swimming pool with its
wonderful views of the port and the
old town.
Calle Pedro Francés 27-9, 07800.
Tel: (971) 31 00 00.
www.ibiza-hotels.com/royal-plaza
La Torre del Canónigo****
You can't beat the location of this
apart-hotel – next door to the cathedral
in Dalt Vila – and the 14th-century
defence tower is a listed building. All
rooms have old-town or harbour views,

air conditioning, satellite TV and DVD,
and there's a sauna and steam room
with whirlpool bath.
Calle Major 8, Dalt Vila.
Tel: (971) 30 38 84. www.elcanonigo.com
Open: Easter–Dec & New Year.

Figueretes
Es Vivé**
A trendy hotel, popular with visiting
DJs working the bars and clubs near
Figueretes and Platja d'en Bossa
beaches. Rooms are airy and pleasant,
if on the small side. Some have sea
views. The bar and restaurant are
good places to hang out, though the
food isn't always up to scratch.
Calle Carles Roman Ferrer 8.
Tel: (971) 30 19 02.
www.hotelesvive.com

Platja d'en Bossa
Hotel Club Goleta****
Large resort hotel, part of the Sirenis
chain. A great place to relax, especially
out of season when it is surprisingly
quiet and prices drop substantially. The
beach is close to hand, the rooms are
comfortable and the amenities
outstanding – spa, sauna, jacuzzi,
swimming pool, table tennis and
billiards.
Avda. Pedro Matutes Noguera s/n.
Tel: (971) 30 21 58.
wwwsirenishotels.com
Torre del Mar****
Luxurious hotel with a convenient
beach location, less than 2km (1.25
miles) from Eivissa. Amenities include
tennis courts, sauna, jacuzzi and
Turkish bath. Disabled access.
Platja d'en Bossa. Tel: (971) 30 30 50.

Platja d'es Figueral
Invisa Hotel Club Cala Blanca**

This large hotel, thoroughly renovated in the 1990s, offers excellent value for money and first-rate sporting facilities, including tennis, archery and water polo. Some rooms have ceiling fans rather than air conditioning.
Platja d'es Figueral, San Carlos.
Tel: (971) 33 51 00.
www.invisa-hoteles.com

Platja Talamanca
Argos***

Sea views are the main draw of this recently refurbished, medium-size hotel between Eivissa and Talamanca bays. All rooms are air-conditioned and of a generous size, and there are two pools, one for children.
Calle La Mola s/n. S'Illa Plana.
Tel: (971) 31 21 62.
Hostal Talamanca **

Modern low-rise building in a quiet location directly overlooking the beach but with shops, bars, restaurants and public transport close to hand.
Platja Talamanca, Apartado 103.
Tel: (971) 31 24 63.
Hotel Lux Isla**

Small hotel only a short walk from the beach but within easy reach of Eivissa. All rooms have satellite TV and most have balconies with sea views.
Calle Josep Pla 1. Tel: (971) 31 34 69.
www.luxisla.com
Victoria Hotel**

The beach-side location of this competitively priced hotel makes it a favourite with families. Most of the rooms have sea views.
Platja Talamanca. Tel: (971) 31 19 12.

Port de Sant Miquel
Galeón***

Now completely refurbished, this large hotel with garden terraces directly overlooking the bay won an architectural award when it first opened in the 1970s. Canoeing, sailing, windsurfing, water-skiing and diving activities are available.
Port de Satn Miquel. Tel: (971) 33 45 34.

Portinatx
El Greco***

Large hotel in a quiet, pine-wooded location overlooking S'Arenal beach with panoramic sea views and a private water park for the children.
Sant Joan de Labritja, 07810.
Tel: (971) 32 05 70.
Hostal Cas Mallorquí**

Nine modern, comfortable rooms with sea views, TV, private bathrooms and air conditioning in a beautiful setting near one of Ibiza's most prized coves. Excellent value.
Cala Es Portixol. Tel: (971) 32 05 05.
Presidente***

Situated in the pine woods above Cala Portinatx, this large tourist hotel with all mod cons is just a short hop from the beach. Handy for exploring other beauty spots such as Xarraca and Sant Miquel.
07810 Sant Joan de Labritja.
Tel: (971) 32 05 75. www.ecohoteles.com

Santa Agnès
Es Cucons****

Currently being considered for agroturisme status, this beautiful 17th-century converted farmhouse enjoys a superb rural setting in the peaceful seclusion of the Ibizan countryside.

Highly recommended.
*2 km (1.25 miles) south west of Santa
Agnès. Tel: (971) 80 55 01.
www.escucons.com*

Santa Eulària des Riu
Buenavista**
Located on the road leading to Puig d'en
Missa, this small hotel, has been in the
hands of the same family since the
1930s. Attractive garden, swimming
pool and bar restaurant.
*San Jaime 1. Tel: (971) 33 00 03.
Open: May–Oct.*
Ca's Català**
Friendly, English-run hotel at the foot of
Puig d'en Missa, close to the restaurants,
shops and beaches of the new town.
Comfortable ensuite rooms and shady
courtyard with small pool and sun
terrace. No children.
*Calle del Sol. Tel: (971) 33 10 06.
www.cascatala.com*
Palladium***
Located near the river in Santa Eulària's
beach 'suburb', this luxury hotel
occupies an historic building inspired by
classic Palladian architecture. Health and
relaxation treatments, including
Thalassotherapy, are the speciality.
*Calle los Lirios 1, Siesta – Santa Eulària
des Riu. Tel: (971) 33 82 60.
www.aaapalladium.com*
Rio Mar**
As the name suggests, this budget hotel
is on the river side of town but within
comfortable walking distance of the
centre. All 120 simply furnished rooms
have ensuite bathrooms and a terrace
with either sea or mountain views.
*Platja els Pins, 07840. Tel: (971) 33 03 27.
www.hotelriomar.com. Open: May–Oct.*

S'Argamassa Palace***
Modern, recently refurbished hotel in
attractive grounds, handily situated for
exploring. There is a decent-sized
swimming pool, a restaurant offering
Mediterranean-style cooking, and
children's playground and garden area.
*Urbanización S'Argamassa s/n.
Tel: (971) 33 02 71.
www.sargamassa-palace.com*
Tres Torres****
Convenience and comfort are the twin
advantages of this modern hotel
overlooking the marina and only three
or 4 minutes' walk to the beach. Sea
views from all rooms.
*Bahía Ses Estaques, 07840.
Tel: (971) 33 03 26. www.ecohoteles.com*

FORMENTERA
Cala Saona
Cala Saona****
The architecture of this standard, sugar-
white modern block may not be
particularly distinguished, but the
location, behind the beach of this
stunning pine-wooded bay, more than
makes up for it. Large, airy rooms, each
with attractive balcony or terrace. The
tennis courts are another plus.
*Cala Saona. Tel: (971) 32 20 30.
Open: Apr–Oct.*

Caló de Sant Agustí
Hostal Residencia Mar Blau**
Excellent budget option near the
fishing harbour and the beach at
Ses Platgetes. Each of the ten
rooms has a terrace with sea views.
Bike and scooter hire available.
*Caló de Sant Agustí. Tel: (971) 32 70 30.
Open: Apr–Oct.*

Es Pujols

Hostal Roca Plana★★

Good value, given the excellent location, overlooking the beach and only 1km (approx. 0.5 mile) from the Ses Salines nature reserve.
Calle Espalmador 41–55, 07860.
Tel: (971) 32 83 35.
www.formentera.net/rocaplana.htm
Open: May–Oct.

Hotel Voramar★★

Friendly hotel close to the beach and the centre of Es Pujols, with shops and restaurants close to hand. Rooms have fans, bath or shower and terrace. Very good value for money.
Avenida Voramar. Tel: (971) 32 81 17.
www.guiaformentera.com/voramar

Sa Volta★★★★

This recently renovated hotel with well-equipped and comfortable rooms looks much better inside than out. Good location on the main street and only a short walk from the beach. The small roof-top pool is another plus.
Miramar 94. Tel: (971) 32 81 25.
www.guiaformentera.com/savolta

Sa Savina

Hostal Bahía★★★

Located in a modern building opposite the marina, the hotel's main asset is its bright, airy, tastefully furnished and spacious rooms, all with air conditioning and TV. Not all have private balconies, but the hotel also has a large terrace.
Passeig de la Marina.
Tel: (971) 32 21 42. www.hbahia.com

Hostal La Savina★★

The location of this popular hostal is near the Estany des Peix (most rooms have lake views) is excellent for anyone wishing to explore the island.
Avda Mediterránea 22–40.
Tel: (971) 32 22 79. Open: May–Oct.

Platja Migjorn

Hostal Costa Azul★★

This hostal enjoys a pleasant pine-shaded setting just behind one of Formentera's most beautiful beaches. Some of the (functional) rooms have sea views, and the Ca Marí restaurant serves delicious, freshly caught fish. Self-catering apartments are also available.
Platja Migjorn apdo 56.
Tel: (971) 32 80 24.
www.illavirtual.com/formentera/users/costaazul

Insotel Club Formentera★★★★

Large hotel (also self-catering studios) in a quiet beach-front location. Extensive gardens. Water sports include scuba diving and sailing.
Platja Migjorn. Tel: (971) 32 80 00.
www.insotel.com

Riu La Mola★★★

Hotel at the La Mola end of Platja Migjorn beach. On-site facilities include gym, tennis courts and mini-golf, with canoe and bike rental also available.
Platja Migjorn. Tel: (971) 32 70 00.
www.riu.com. Open: May–Oct.

Platja de Sa Roqueta

Lago Playa ★★★

Small hotel near the beach at sa Roqueta and within easy reach (1km (0.5 mile)) of Es Pujols.
Platja sa Roqueta.
Tel: (971) 32 85 07.

Sant Ferran
Apartamentos Mayans**
Seven apartments, each with a private terrace in an attractive building near the centre of the village. Well situated for exploring the island, with Es Pujols and Platja Migjorn both close to hand.
Ctra. Cala En Baster 3km, 07871.
Tel: (971) 32 84 39.
*www.illavirtual.com/formentera/users/
mayans*

AGROTURISME
Cala Jondal
Can Jondal****
There are fabulous views from this old farmhouse in a romantic setting, 9km (5.5 miles) southeast of Sant Josep and within easy reach of Cala Jondal. Pamper yourself with a massage, acupuncture or reiki.
Cala Jondal.
Tel: (971) 18 72 70.

Eivissa
Can Pere Mari***
Golfing enthusiasts will love this sensitively converted 19th-century farmhouse nestling in delightful countryside only a short drive from the capital and not far (9km (5.5 miles)) from Santa Eulària. Facilities include a swimming pool, but there is no restaurant.
On the Cala Llonga road, 1km (approx. 0.5 mile) west of Roca Llisa golf course.
Tel: (971) 18 71 34.
www.canperemari.com

Sant Carles
Can Curreu****
This converted farmhouse enjoys a peaceful wooded setting in the hills to the west of Las Dalias. The restaurant serves excellent food and the facilities include a jacuzzi, swimming pool, gym and solarium. Horse riding and power-boat excursions are also available.
Aptdo. de Correos 240 (off the Es Canar road, west of Sant Carles at km 12).
Tel: (971) 33 52 80.
www.cancurreu.com

Sant Joan
Can Marti**
This family-run organic farm, in a beautiful valley overlooked by hills planted with olives, almonds and carob trees, is within comfortable walking distance of the village. The centuries-old house hs been renovated, but retains its charm. Home-produced fruit and vegetables are available, likewise organic breakfasts. Magnificent beaches can be accessed within a short drive.
1km (approx. 0.5 mile) west of Sant Joan.
Tel: (971) 33 35 00.
www.canmarti.com Open: Mar–Oct.

Santa Agnès
Can Pujolet****
This early 20th-century farmhouse, converted to suit 21st-century tastes, is situated in the hills to the northeast of the village and is the perfect location for mountain-biking and horse-riding. Cala d'en Sardinia, one of the island's more remote coves, is temptingly close, but getting to the hotel pool (with jacuzzi) is a less strenuous option. Breakfast is included but there is no restaurant. All rooms feature a terrace.
2.5km (1.5 miles) northeast of Santa Agnès. Tel: (971) 80 51 70.
www.ibizarural.com

Practical Guide

Arriving
Entry formalities

Visitors from the EU can enter Spain without a visa providing they have a valid national identity card or passport (valid for at least 3 months after the intended date of leaving the island). Citizens of Canada, New Zealand, the USA and Australia do not need a visa for short stays. It is advisable to consult with a tour company, airline or consulate before travelling.

By air

Most visitors arrive by charter flights as part of a package holiday. Iberia and Air Europa have scheduled flights to Ibiza via Madrid, Barcelona and other Spanish airports. Bear in mind that flights are heavily booked during the holiday season. The flight from the UK takes around 2.5 hours.

Air Europa. *Tel: (0870) 240 1501. www.air-europa.com*

Iberia. *Tel: (902) 400 500. www.iberia.com*

Ibiza's international airport is at Sant Jordi, 7km (4 miles) south west of Eivissa. Facilities include a tourist office (May–September only), cash points and car rental. Plans to expand the airport are meeting considerable resistance from local residents.

Ibiza airport. *Tel: (971) 80 90 00.* There is an hourly bus service to Eivissa town centre. Journey time is about 30 minutes, and the last trip leaves at 10.30pm. The taxi ride takes 15 minutes.

Lapping up the sunshine, Ibiza style

By ferry
There are regular services to Ibiza from the Spanish mainland and via Mallorca. The main companies are:
Baleària. *Tel: (902) 191 068.*
www.balearia.com
Trasmediterránea. *Tel: (902) 454 645.*
www.trasmediterranea.es
Umafisa. *Tel: (902) 160 180.*
www.umafisa.com

Camping
There are only a handful of campsites in Ibiza and none at all in Formentera. All are open Easter to late-October only. Camping outside the official areas (including beaches) is illegal.

Camping Cala Bassa. Near the beach, with all facilities. *Tel: (971) 34 45 99.*

Camping Cala Nova. 100m from the beach and equally convenient for Es Canar. *Tel: (971) 33 17 74.*

Children
Children up to the age of 12 travel half-price on public transport. Infants travel free.

It is not advisable to bring babies younger than 2 years during July and August because of the heat. Most hotels offer a babysitting service. If you have a baby monitor with you, you will need to buy an adaptor, which is available in local supermarkets. Some hotels provide all-day care and special entertainment for youngsters.

Climate and what to wear
Pack light, airy clothes for July and August as it is usually hot at night too. In May, June and September it starts to get a little cooler in the evenings, so a light

jacket or jumper is a good idea. Bring a waterproof, as the odd shower is always a possibility. While the climate from October to April is generally mild, you will need a jumper and waterproof jacket.

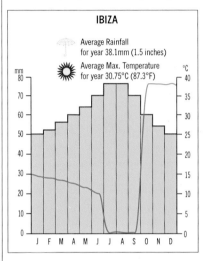

IBIZA

Average Rainfall
for year 38.1mm (1.5 inches)

Average Max. Temperature
for year 30.75°C (87.3°F)

Consulates
Australia. The nearest consulate is in Barcelona: *Gran Via Carles III 98. Tel: (093) 330 9496.*

Canada. The nearest consulate is in Barcelona: *Via Augusta 125. Tel: (093) 209 0634. www.canada-es.org*

UK. *Avda Isidoro Macabich 45, 1 Eivissa. Tel: (971) 30 18 16.*

USA. The nearest consulate is in Palma de Mallorca: *Edificio Reina Constanza, Porto Pi, 8, 9-D, 07015 Palma de Mallorca, Spain. Tel: (971) 40 37 07 or 40 39 05. www.embusa.es*

Crime and safety
Crime is not a major problem in Ibiza. There is little street violence, and women are generally able to walk

Riding a scooter is an enjoyable way to explore the islands

appropriate consulate. It's a good idea to keep a separate list of passport details, traveller's cheque numbers, holiday insurance policy numbers and credit card emergency phone numbers.

Customs regulations

The duty-free allowance for visitors to Spain is 800 cigarettes or 200 cigars, 10 litres of spirits and 90 litres of wine, 20 litres of fortified wine, 110 litres of beer, 60 centilitres of perfume and 230 centilitres of toilet water. Non-EU residents may apply for VAT refunds on duty-free for tourists' goods: to do this you will need a *formulari*, stamped by a customs officer as you leave. The refund can be claimed at the airport, by post or via a bank transfer.

Driving

To drive in Ibiza you need a full EU licence which you must carry with you at all times, together with your passport and all insurance and car-hire documentation. The Spanish drive on the right. Traffic on a roundabout has priority from the left. Speed limits are as follows: 120km/h (75mph) on motorways, 90km/h (56mph) on major roads and 50km/h (31mph) in towns. Children under 14 must travel in the back seat, and seat belts are compulsory at all times. The local police are vigilant

around safely at night. Thefts do occur wherever there are crowds – in airports, bus stations, around major tourist attractions and even in some hotels, so you need to take sensible precautions. Leave nothing valuable visible in a parked car, avoid carrying excessive amounts of cash and never leave handbags or wallets unattended on tables or on the backs of chairs. Where possible, leave valuables in an insured safety deposit box in your hotel or apartment. Report any loss to the police, who will give you a *denuncia* (written statement) which you need to keep for insurance claims. Lost or stolen passports should be reported to the

and enforce drink-driving and other regulations, with random checks and hefty on-the-spot fines. Penalties for serious drink-driving offences have recently been increased. Outside the main towns, petrol pumps are few and far between, so make sure you fill up before setting off. It makes little sense to drive in the towns. Historic areas like Dalt Vila in Eivissa are closed to motor traffic, making for congestion elsewhere. Pavements marked with a blue line are designated pay-park areas. The system works on a 'pay and display' basis. Do not exceed the time indicated, as traffic wardens are 'clamp happy' and fines are prohibitive. Parking is usually free from 2–4pm and after 10pm, but check the schedules on the machines.

Hiring a car, motorcycle or scooter (a very popular option) opens up the possibility of exploring the furthest reaches of Ibiza in a relatively short space of time – no destination is further than 45km (28 miles). Cars are discouraged on Formentera for environmental reasons. To rent a car you must be over 21 and have held a full licence for at least 2 years. Check insurance cover for accident, vehicle theft and liability before you sign on the dotted line. The law requires that all cars carry a red warning triangle and replacement headlamp bulbs. Ask the rental company to confirm that these comply with regulations.

Avis, **Hertz** and **Europcar** have desks at the airport, but the local firms offer cheaper rates.

Rent a Car: pick-up and return service at the airport, with a wide range of cars. *Tel: (971) 34 05 21.*

Calle de Pere Tur, Dalt Vila

Electricity

The voltage is 220v. Mains sockets need the European two-pin plugs.

Emergency telephone numbers

General emergencies (all services) 112. Red Cross emergency ambulance (971) 29 50 00.

Health

Avoid the beach between 1pm and 4pm. Always use a high-factor sun block (don't forget to apply it to your feet) and make use of hired umbrellas. Re-apply sun block after going in the water – no sun cream is 100 per cent waterproof. Children should always wear T-shirts and hats. Other beach illnesses include heat rash (caused by too much tanning product), dizziness, sore throat and upset tummy (caused by downing iced drinks in the sun). Local water is safe to drink, but bottled water tastes better. Doctors offer emergency care of the kind found in accident and emergency units in the UK, and basic medical advice and help can be

Ibiza's crystal clear waters are a paradise for snorkellers

provided by pharmacists (*farmacia*: look for the green cross, which is lit when the shop is open). Pharmacists display a list of which branch is open when, and in the resorts most pharmacists speak some English, so communication should not be a problem.

Hospitals and Health Centres (*Centre de Salut*):

Eivissa, Hospital Can Misses, *Carrer de Corona. Tel: (971) 39 70 00 / 64.*

Santa Eulària Health Centre, *Carrer Marià Riquer Wallis 4. Tel: (971) 33 24 53.*

Sant Antoni Health Centre, *Carrer d'Alacant 33. Tel: (971) 34 51 02.*

Red Cross (*Cruz Roja*), *Avda Espanya, Eivissa. Tel: (971) 3 9 03 03.*

Formentera Health Centre, *Ctra La Savina-Sant Francesc 3.1km. Tel: (971) 32 23 57.*

Insurance

EU citizens are entitled to free emergency medical treatment – take with you an E111 (obtainable from post offices). All visitors should also arrange insurance to cover non-urgent treatments and the costs of repatriation.

Maps

Make sure your map is marked in Catalan, as many signs are in Catalan not Spanish.

Tourist information offices have town plans and maps of suggested hiking, cycling and driving routes. For hiking or cycling, the most detailed maps are produced by the Instituto Geográfica Nacional and are obtainable from specialist bookshops including Transit, *Carrer d'Arago 45, Eivissa.*

GENERAL VOCABULARY

yes	sí
no	no
please	por favor
thank you	gracias
You're welcome	de nada
hello	hola
goodbye	adiós
good morning/day	buenos días
good afternoon	buenas tardes
good evening/night	buenas noches
excuse me	¡disculpe!
Sorry	lo siento
Help!	¡socorro!
today	hoy
tomorrow	mañana
yesterday	ayer

USEFUL WORDS AND PHRASES

open	abierto
closed	cerrado
push	empujar
pull	tirar
How much is it?	¿Cuánto es?
expensive	carola
bank	el banco

bureau de change	la oficina de cambio
post office	correos
duty chemist	la farmacia de guardia
bank card	la tarjeta de banco
credit card	la tarjeta de crédito
traveller's cheques	los cheques de viaje
table	la mesa
menu	el menú/la carta
waiter	el/la camarerola
water	agua
fizzy/still water	agua con/sin gas
I don't understand	no entiendo
The bill, please	La cuenta, por favor
Do you speak English?	¿Habla usted inglés?
My name is...	Me llamo…
Where are the toilets?	¿Dónde están los servicios?
Where is there a telephone?	¿Dónde está un teléfono?
Can you call me a taxi?	¿Puede llamar a un taxi?
Can you help me?	¿Puede ayudarme?

Media

Many pubs and cafés have satellite TV (BBC, Sky etc), usually catering for sports fans.

Ibiza has no local English-language newspapers; however, international editions of British and German newspapers are available.

Money matters

The unit of currency is the euro. Notes range from 5–500 euros, coins from 1 céntimo to 2 euros. Euro coins and bank notes from other countries are all acceptable currency.

Multilingual ATMs are commonplace in the main towns but more of a rarity in the smaller seaside resorts and remoter villages. Most hotels,

To avoid disappointment check opening times of museums and monuments before setting out

Police

There are three police forces in Ibiza: The Policía Nacional (state police) deal with serious incidents; the Policía Municipal (local police) patrol the small towns and resorts; and the Guardia Civil (National Guard) operate mostly in rural areas.
Eivissa *Tel: (971) 31 58 61.*
Sant Antoni *Tel: (971) 34 08 30/34 39 11.*
Santa Eulària *Tel: (971) 33 08 40.*

restaurants and shops accept credit cards, though pensions, hostals, smaller cafés and market stalls may insist on payment in cash. Bear in mind that if you are changing traveller's cheques, banks close at 2pm. Exchange rates are poorer in hotels and bureaux de change.

Opening hours

Museums and historic monuments are usually open Tue–Sun 10am–2pm and 4–6pm, but closed on public holidays and fiestas. Times are often reduced in the winter.

Offices work similar hours. Big department stores tend to open all day from 8 or 9am to 6pm, while many shops in the resorts remain open till late at night.

Banks are open Mon–Fri 9am–2pm, Sat 9am–1pm.

Post offices

Postal services from the islands often take some time to reach their destination. If a message is urgent, use fax or e-mail. The express (*urgente*) deliveries are not always as quick as they claim to be.

Post offices are generally open Mon–Sat 9am–2pm, 5–7pm. Stamps can also be bought from hotel desks and from tobacconists (*Tabacos*). Post boxes are yellow.

The central post office is on *Avenida Isidor Macabich 76, Eivissa.*

Public holidays

1 January *Año Nuevo* New Year's Day
6 January *Día de los Reyes* Epiphany
1 March *Día de les Illes Balears* Balearic Self-Government Day
March/April (variable)
Viernes Santo Good Friday
1 May *Día del Trabajo* Labour Day

Eivissa at dusk

May/June (variable) Corpus Christi
25 July *Sant Jaume* Feast of St James
(Formentera only)
8 August *Sant Ciriac* (Eivissa only)
15 August *Asuncíon de la virgen*
Assumption of the Blessed Virgin Mary
12 October *Día de la Hispanidad*

National Day of Spain
1 November *Todos los Santos* All Saints'
Day
6 December *Día de la Constitucíon*
Constitution Day
8 December *Inmaculada Concepcíon*
Immaculate Conception
25 December *Día de
Navidad* Christmas Day

Public transport
Buses

The main bus station in
Ibiza is in Eivissa (*Avda
Isidor Macabich*). There is
a café here if you have to
wait for a bus. Tickets are
sold in advance from the
windows, where
timetables and prices are
posted. Few of the staff
speak English, so it may
be necessary to write
down your destination.
Bear in mind that most

Tourists are lured by the charms of the street stalls at Sant Antoni

FERRY TRIPS

Boat services to Formentera (La Savina) depart from Sant Antoni and Santa Eulària in season, but the service is much less frequent than from Eivissa (departure estacion maritima, Av. Santa Eulària). The cheapest option is the ferry (journey time approximately 75 minutes) but if you want to maximise your stay, you can set off earlier (7.45am) and return later (8pm) on the hydrofoil (35 minutes). Bear in mind, however, that this is nearly twice as expensive.

place names are still written in Spanish. This causes most confusion with Eivissa (Pueblo Ibiza). Buses link Eivissa to the main towns. The sign 'P' means *parada* (stop). In Sant Antoni the main bus terminus is opposite the ferry port. There are half-hourly services from here to Eivissa (Pueblo Ibiza on the timetable), via Sant Rafel and Sant Josef, and good connections to Port des Torrent and other nearby beaches.

A disco bus service operates hourly from midnight to dawn with routes linking all the clubs. It is much cheaper than the taxi but buses get very crowded in August and you may have to wait. Autocares Paya operate a bus service which connects La Savina with the main villages on Formentera.

Information can be found at *www.ibizabus.com*

Ferries

Local ferries run (summer only) from Eivissa to Playa d'en Bossa and between Eivissa, Es Cana, Cala Llonga and Santa Eulària. In Sant Antoni there are shuttle services to Port des Torrent and other local beaches.

Taxis

Taxis are white with a diagonal stripe on both front doors. Taxis for hire always display a green light. Charges are fixed according to the length of the journey: a list of tariffs is displayed at ranks and is available from tourist offices, and you should always check the price before starting the journey. A proposal to introduce meters is still being discussed. Taxis to the airport charge an additional tariff.

Taxis are plentiful and journeys are competitively priced

Radio Taxi Eivissa. *Tel: (971) 39 84 83.*
Santa Eulària. *Tel: (971) 33 30 33.*
Sant Antoni. *Tel: (971) 34 37 64.*

Telephones
Public telephones, coin- or card-
operated, can be found in kiosks and in
bars and restaurants. Phone cards are
sold in tobacconists. There are two types
– one with a black magnetic strip, the
other with a PIN number. Local calls are
cheap. The most economical option for
phoning abroad is the international
phone card. International calls are
cheapest at night – between 10pm and
8am and on Sundays.
   The code for Spain is 0034.
   The code for the Balearic islands is
971 – dial all nine digits when making
a call.
   To call the UK dial 0044 then the
number, excluding the first zero.

Time
Ibiza, like the rest of Spain, is on Central
European Time, one hour ahead of
GMT (Greenwich Mean Time).

Tipping
Five to ten per cent is customary in bars
and restaurants unless a service charge
has already been taken.

Toilets
Public toilets are few and far between.
Use the facilities in cafés, bars and
restaurants whenever possible, but only
if you are a customer.

Tourist Information
Spanish Tourist Board:
Australia: *1st floor 178 Collin's Street,*

Melbourne. Tel: (03) 9650 7377.
Canada: *2 Bloor Street West, 34th floor,*
Toronto M4W 3E2. Tel: (416) 961 3131 .
UK: *22–23 Manchester Square, London,*
W1M 5AP. Tel: (020) 7486 8077.
USA: *666 5th Avenue, 35th floor, New*
York, NY 10103. Tel: (212) 265 8822.
   There is a tourist information desk at
the airport. (*Open May–Sept.*
Tel: (971) 80 91 18.)
   Tourist Offices in the major resorts
generally open 10am–2pm, 4–6pm.
Smaller offices close during the
winter.
   Eivissa: *Vara de Rey 13, Eivissa. Tel:*
(971) 3019 00. Fax: (971) 30 15 62.
E-mail: IB.Mintour05@bitel.es
   Oficina de Turismo Sant Antoni,
Paseo de Ses Fonts, Sant Antoni de
Portmany. Tel: (971) 34 33 63.
Fax: (971) 34 41 75.
   Santa Eulària: *Mariano Riquer Wallis,*
Santa Eulària. Tel: (971) 33 07 28.
Fax: (971) 33 29 59.
   S'Illot: *Llevant 7, Sant Llorenç S'Illot.*
Tel/fax: (971) 81 06 99.

Travellers with disabilities
Spain lags behind many European
countries in this respect. Most hotels,
museums and shops are difficult, if not
impossible, to access, as is public
transport, although some buses are
now being provided with ramps. For
further advice contact: The Federació
ECOM (The Catalan Association for the
Disabled), *Gran Via de les Corts*
Catalanes 562, principal 2a Barcelona.
Tel: (934) 51 55 50, or the COCEMFE
(The Spanish Association for the
Disabled) *Calle Luis Cabrera 63, Madrid.*
Tel: (917) 44 36 00.